RECKONING WITH REA

P9-DVZ-603

Reckoning with Reagan

Reckoning with Reagan

America and Its President in the 1980s

MICHAEL SCHALLER

New York   Oxford
OXFORD UNIVERSITY PRESS
1992

Oxford University Press

Oxford   New York   Toronto
Delhi   Bombay   Calcutta   Madras   Karachi
Petaling Jaya   Singapore   Hong Kong   Tokyo
Nairobi   Dar es Salaam   Cape Town
Melbourne   Auckland

and associated companies in

Berlin   Ibadan

Copyright © 1992 by Oxford University Press, Inc.

Published by Oxford University Press, Inc.
200 Madison Avenue, New York, New York 10016

Oxford is a registered trademark of Oxford University Press

Library of Congress Cataloging-in-Publication Data
Schaller, Michael, 1947–
Reckoning with Reagan : America and its president
in the 1980s / Michael Schaller.
p.   cm.   Includes bibliographical references and index.
ISBN 0-19-506915-3
1. United States—Politics and government—1981–1989.
2. Reagan, Ronald.   I. Title.
E876.S29   1992   973.927—dc20   91-38021

1 3 5 7 9 8 6 4 2

Printed in the United States of America
on acid-free paper

For my mother,
Edith Schaller,
and the memory of my father,
Lawrence Schaller

Preface

Ronald Reagan left office on January 20, 1989, as one of the most popular presidents of the twentieth century. Since then, the demise of communism as a global force and the disappearance of the Soviet Union as a unified nation and military superpower have added lustre to the accomplishments of his administration. Reagan's domestic programs also won favor from the electorate. He came into office pledging to increase defense spending, curtail welfare programs, reduce taxes, and change the liberal direction of the U.S. Supreme Court. To a considerable extent, he accomplished these goals.

A relatively short time has elapsed since Reagan left office, and it seems an appropriate moment for a historian to make an initial evaluation of the Reagan presidency and its impact on the United States. Several journalists, including Haynes Johnson and Lou Cannon, have published impressive accounts of the Reagan years. More than a score of administration "insiders"—presidential aides and Reagan family members—have also produced a valuable memoir literature. In addition, a wide array of academic specialists have published detailed accounts of particular policies and events transpiring between 1981 and 1989. These sources, noted in the Bibliography, provide a starting point for interpreting this period.

Despite the early appearance of so many personal and journalistic accounts, Ronald Reagan remains an elusive figure. Administration insiders, as well as critics, often found it difficult to say precisely what he believed. Even one of his favorite speechwriters, Peggy Noonan, who deeply admired the president, described his brain as "barren terrain." As Donald Regan, first his Secretary of the Treasury and then White House Chief of Staff, observed, performing persuasively was "second nature" to the president and a key to Reagan's political success. He had been "learning his lines, composing his facial expressions, hitting his toe marks for half a century." Like the dialogue he spoke in more than a dozen movies of the 1930s and 1940s, Reagan's presidential assertions sounded utterly sincere and evoked broad agreement among Americans.

The president understood the importance of his professional background and enjoyed repeating popular lines of dialogue from fellow actors like Clint Eastwood. It is anybody's guess how many times he challenged Democrats to "go ahead," pass a spending bill, and "make my day." Recalling his youthful role as football player George Gipp in *Knute Rockne—All American,* he often rallied the public against Congress by asking their help to "win one for the Gipper."

In his own breezy account of his presidency, published soon after he left office, Reagan described the joy he felt leaving Washington as often as possible to vacation at his California ranch. Although he stopped short of claiming he had been born in a log cabin, the president described the solace he found in clearing brush and splitting logs. In this wild "real" America, he explained, "having a horse between my knees . . . ma[de] it easier to sort out a problem."

Reagan's invariably upbeat and unreflective accounts of his life and presidency prompted biographer Garry Wills to describe him as "Mr. Magoo." Like the kindly, bumbling, myopic cartoon character, Reagan lived a politically charmed life in a world he thought he fully controlled but only dimly understood. Eventually, access to official records will permit a more thorough and dispassionate evaluation of this period. In the interim, I offer these insights.

I wish to thank Nancy Lane, my editor at Oxford University Press, for her enthusiastic support of this project. Robert D.

Schulzinger, of the University of Colorado, and Leonard Dinner-stein, my colleague at Arizona, read the full manuscript with great care. Virginia Scharff, of the University of New Mexico, commented on portions of the material. Their criticism has made this, I hope, a better book.

Tucson, Ariz.   M.S.
December 1991

Contents

Reckoning with Reagan

1

The Man on Horseback

As CITIZEN and president, Ronald Reagan had an abiding vision of America which could be characterized as either idealistic or naive. Shortly after leaving office, he revealed an unfulfilled dream of taking his Soviet counterpart, Mikhail Gorbachev, "up in a helicopter to show him how Americans lived." Reagan would point out an ordinary factory, "its parking lot filled with workers' cars, then we'd fly over a residential neighborhood and I'd tell him that's where those workers lived—in homes with lawns and backyards, perhaps with a second car or a boat in the driveway." The president imagined landing and knocking at a front door so Gorbachev could "ask the people how they live and what they think of our system." Of course, he noted, America's true greatness lay less in material riches than in its values that gave preeminence to individual freedom.

If suburban subdivisions represented one pole of Reagan's America, what he called the "wild scenery and serenity" of the West formed another. Throughout his presidency, the rustic "Rancho del Cielo" in the mountains outside Santa Barbara, California, served as a sanctuary from the urban and political squalor of Washington. Reagan spent nearly a full year of vacation time on his ranch during his eight years as president. There he and his wife Nancy could "put on our boots and old clothes, recharge our batteries, and be reminded of where we had come from." It was a lot

3

easier for him to "sort out a problem," Reagan explained, when he had a "horse between my knees." Small wonder the Secret Service gave him the codename "Rawhide."

The clashing symbols of well-tended lawns and rough-hewed cowboys evoked recognition and empathy from a large majority of Americans. At the height of Reagan's popularity in 1986, *Time* magazine wrote admiringly of how he had "found America's sweet spot." Describing his activities during the July 4 holiday as he unveiled a refurbished Statue of Liberty in New York harbor, *Time* gushed about how the 75-year-old man was "hitting home runs . . . with triumphant (some might even say careless or even callous) ease that is astonishing and even mysterious." Reagan was a "magician who carries a bright, ideal America like a holograph in his mind and projects its image in the air."

Not since journalist Theodore White rhapsodized about "Camelot" in the wake of John F. Kennedy's assassination had a president been spoken of so reverently. In the interim, the Vietnam War, Watergate scandal, economic decline, and Iranian hostage crisis had tarnished the presidencies of Lyndon Johnson, Richard Nixon, Gerald Ford, and Jimmy Carter. All had left office disgraced.

In 1980, the collapse of detente with the Soviet Union, rampant inflation, and the unresolved fate of American captives in Iran doomed the Carter administration and energized the candidacy of Ronald Reagan. Downplaying his conservative economic and social ideas, the Republican nominee called for a restoration of national strength and pride. "This is the greatest country in the world," he declared, "we have the talent, we have the drive, we have the imagination. Now all we need is the leadership." Promising to bring the public a "little good news," Reagan ridiculed those who suggested "that the United States has had its day in the sun."

In his inaugural address on January 20, 1981, President Reagan scoffed at those who spoke of a national "malaise." It was "time for us to realize that we are too great a nation to limit ourselves to small dreams." Reagan paid homage to heroes of past wars and stressed a few easily understood economic grievances, such as inflation and a burdensome tax system. Playing to the widely held disillusion with public policy, he declared that "in this present crisis, government is not the solution to our problem, government is the problem."

Over the next eight years, through recession and economic recovery, cold war and detente, Ronald Reagan forged a powerful bond with the public. Even when a majority of citizens opposed specific administration programs, such as its efforts to ban abortion, support anti-communist guerrillas in Central America, and cut school aid, most continued to express confidence in the president. Reagan's popularity seemed so unrelated to success and so undiminished even by failure or scandal that Colorado Representative Pat Schroeder dubbed Reagan the "Teflon president."

Veteran Democrats like Clark Clifford and House Speaker Thomas "Tip" O'Neill dismissed Reagan as an "amiable dunce," more suitable as a ceremonial king than a president. Journalists chronicled weekly presidential gaffes, such as blaming redwood trees for air pollution or insisting that nuclear missiles could be recalled after launching. One irate scholar complained that Reagan was the "first modern president whose contempt for the facts is treated as a charming idiosyncracy." But television commentator Bill Moyers hit nearer the mark when he observed that "we didn't elect this guy because he knows how many barrels of oil are in Alaska. We elected him because we want to feel good."

Roots

To those who noticed him in 1964, Ronald Reagan seemed a washed up 53-year-old actor. Although still handsome and financially secure, he had recently lost his job as a motivational speaker and television host for the General Electric Company. For nearly a decade he had been employed to speak before thousands of GE workers, chambers of commerce, and community groups in his capacity as a "corporate ambassador of goodwill."

Born in Tampico, Illinois, on February 6, 1911, Reagan grew to maturity in the nearby town of Dixon, along the Mississippi River. He described his early years as "one of those rare Huck Finn-Tom Sawyer idylls." Those familiar with Mark Twain's novels know they chronicle racism, violence, drunkenness, and superstition in mid-nineteenth-century America. Reagan remembered the ideal-ized Hollywood renditions of Twain, not the genuine article. In the view of one biographer, Reagan subtly distorted his memory "toward small perfections, like the buildings in Disneyland."

As the younger son of an alcoholic father and a religiously fer-vent (Disciples of Christ) mother, the future president's childhood resembled Twain's novels in ways he preferred to forget. Reagan's father Jack had difficulty keeping his job as a shoe salesman and the family moved frequently, often just ahead of the bill collector. Nelle Reagan encouraged her son to act in school plays, an activity in which he exhibited much talent. Despite his insistence that he lived a pleasant childhood, Reagan's favorite White House speech-writer, Peggy Noonan, "had the feeling he came from a sad house" and for the rest of his life "thought it was his job to cheer everyone up."

Early on, "Dutch" (a nickname given Ronald by his father that he retained until he went to Hollywood) Reagan created a distance between the reality of his experience and his feelings by focusing on the ideals and the mythology of American culture. His favorite childhood books included biographies of sports heroes, Edgar Rice Burroughs' fantasy novels, and Horatio Alger-type stories about midwestern boys whose pluck and luck made them respectable. Among his favorites he counted *That Printer of Udell's,* by Harold Bell Wright, in which a young printer attends night school and is rewarded by marrying a beautiful socialite.

More fortunate than many of his contemporaries, Reagan at-tended the religiously affiliated Eureka College during the early years of the Great Depression. After the election of Franklin D. Roosevelt in 1933, the unemployed Jack Reagan found work with a New Deal work-relief program. In appreciation, Dutch became a fervent supporter of Roosevelt, memorizing many of the presi-dent's speeches and doing FDR impersonations for friends. Al-though Roosevelt always remained in Reagan's pantheon, it was as an inspirational hero rather than as the architect of the New Deal and the modern welfare state.

After graduating from Eureka in 1932, Reagan got a job as a radio announcer with station WOC in Davenport, Iowa. His voice, which projected warmth and sincerity, soon brought him a promotion to the job of sports announcer with station WHO in Des Moines. Reagan narrated recreations of baseball games that came into the station via telegraph. He mixed colorful details and folksy anecdotes so well that many listeners preferred his fictional narrations to live coverage.

Reagan's life resembled the good fortune of the Horatio Alger characters he admired. In 1937, while in California to cover the spring training of the Chicago Cubs, he took a screen test for the Warner Brothers' Studio and won a contract. During the next four years his career as a player in so-called B films blossomed. He took direction well, learned lines easily, and was popular among both fellow actors and studio executives. In 1940 he married actress Jane Wyman.

The years before the Pearl Harbor attack were personally and professionally fulfilling ones. Reagan enjoyed playing light, romantic leads and adventure roles. His one complaint with the studio was its refusal to cast him in many westerns. On screen, he often portrayed characters who responded to danger or adversity with a wisecrack followed by a "pep talk." Gradually, his off-screen personality resembled his casting.

His most memorable films in this period include *Knute Rockne— All American* and *King's Row*. In the former, an inspirational fantasy, Reagan played Notre Dame football hero George Gipp. In a fictional deathbed statement, Gipp tells coach Rockne: "Someday when the team is in trouble . . . tell them to win one for the Gipper." Reagan liked the line so much he later made it a trademark of political speeches.

King's Row, probably Reagan's best film, differed markedly from most of his romantic leads. It told the harrowing story of a young man (played by Reagan) whose legs are amputated needlessly by the vengeful doctor-father of a girl he had courted. As the character awoke from surgery and realized what had happened, he screamed "Where's the rest of me?" The line haunted Reagan for years, eventually inspiring the title of the ghostwritten memoir he published in 1965.

Soon after the United States entered the Second World War, Reagan joined millions of other Americans in the armed forces. Ineligible for combat because of his poor eyesight, he served in an

Army Air Corps film unit based in Hollywood. He lived at home while producing army morale films. Several of his pictures depicted war as a form of entertainment, as in *This Is the Army* where Reagan played a corporal staging a variety show. At the end of the film, the recruits march off to battle singing in harmony. These wartime films, with their fictional tales of heroism and comradery, imprinted themselves indelibly on Reagan's memory. For example, he frequently told the fanciful story of how segregation in the armed forces ended the day Japan attacked Pearl Harbor. In the midst of battle, Reagan explained, a black sailor aboard a crippled battleship came up from the galley, "cradled a machine gun in his arms . . . and blazed away at Japanese airplanes." Inspired by this courage, military commanders ended discrimination. Reporter Lou Cannon, who covered Reagan as governor of California and as president, once asked him why, if segregation had ended in 1941, President Harry S Truman had to issue an order in 1948 to end it. Reagan insisted, "I remember the scene, it was very powerful."

Several times during the 1980 campaign Reagan brought himself and audiences to tears describing, in a quivering voice, the tale of a pilot who sacrificed his life—and won a posthumous Congressional Medal of Honor—cradling a wounded comrade rather than bail out from his crippled plane. "Never mind, son," the pilot tells the injured belly gunner, "we'll ride this one down together." Reagan seemed puzzled when journalists questioned how he could possibly know what two dead men said to each other moments before a crash. No medal was every awarded for such an incident. Again, a montage of scenes from several wartime films appears to have inspired the story.

At some level Reagan probably felt self-conscious about his own wartime service. He told a biographer in the 1960s that when he got out of the Army Air Corps "all I wanted to do—in common with several million other veterans—was to rest up awhile, make love to my wife, and come up refreshed to do a better job in an ideal world." This obscured the fact that unlike most of the "several million other veterans," Reagan had left neither home nor wife while in military service.

In 1983, he again embellished his wartime record by confusing it with a movie. This time he told at least two groups that he had firsthand experience with the Holocaust because he had filmed the liberation of Nazi death camps in Europe while in the Signal Corps. When journalists noted that Reagan had not set foot outside the United States during the war, a White House spokesman released an explanation that the president meant to say that he had been greatly affected by seeing a film about death camps after the war ended.

These misstatements, probably not intended to deceive, suggest the depth of Reagan's belief in myths of individual heroism and how he longed to be part of a larger, shared experience—in this case the triumph over fascism in the Second World War. They also revealed his tenacity in holding firm to an idea once he had convinced himself it was true. Throughout his public career, Reagan told stories of pilgrims, patriots, cowboys, and rugged individualists who existed more in movie scripts than in real life. In evoking these symbols, he came across as sincere and persuasive in large part because, like all good salesmen, he truly believed in whatever he said.

While Reagan's film career stagnated after 1945, that of Jane Wyman flourished. Personal and professional tensions led Wyman to divorce him in 1949. She received custody of their two young children, Michael (who had been adopted) and Maureen. During this difficult period Reagan became increasingly active in the Screen Actors Guild (SAG), a union. He served first as board member and then as president from 1947–1952.

Like many Americans during the early postwar years, Reagan's antipathy toward fascism and Hitler gave way to anxiety about communism and the Soviet threat. The Cold War at home and abroad increasingly shaped Reagan's political consciousness. As early as 1946, he later reported, he recognized "the Communist plan" of sending their "first team" to "take over the motion picture business" as part of Stalin's plot to brainwash Americans. In fact, Communists had minuscule influence in Hollywood during the 1940s. They did participate actively in union drives and several talented screenwriters had communist affiliations. But when studio executives were asked by congressional investigators to cite examples of Red influence, they did little more than point to scripts that showed Indians or African-Americans in sympathetic scenes.

Reagan has written that anonymous Communists threatened to attack him while he served as president of SAG. Out of concern, he began carrying a gun. His views of the Red threat often mirrored movie plots. For example, he sometimes described Hollywood Communists as "our little red brothers," comparing them to renegade Indians in a western film. Reagan testified as a "friendly witness" before the House Committee on Un-American Activities, and endorsed efforts to purge the film industry of Communists. He accepted the Hollywood studios' blacklisting of left-wing actors and, on occasion, met secretly with FBI agents to report on the political affiliations of Hollywood personalities. In 1952, Reagan married Nancy Davis, a bit player under contract to MGM. A devoted wife who gave up her career, over the next few years she bore two children, Patricia and Ronald, Jr. Reagan's fading film career took a prosperous turn in 1954 when General Electric hired him to host its weekly television series and deliver corporate speeches.

As host, performer, and part-time producer of the General Electric Theater, as well as corporate "ambassador of goodwill," Reagan's life during the 1950s centered on activities arranged by the giant consumer products company. General Electric remodeled the Reagan residence in California, turning it into a living advertisement for the "all electric home." The Reagans made television commercials that both sold appliances and stimulated a desire to live the kind of life that created a demand for electric gadgets. Over an eight-year period, Reagan visited GE plants throughout the country, meeting with executives, assembly-line workers, and local chambers of commerce. His several thousand after-dinner presentations invariably included an ode to "traditional values," an alarm about contemporary threats, and entertaining anecdotes. Year after year, Reagan warned of communism abroad and creeping socialism at home. He told audiences that "the individual was, and should be forever, the master of his destiny." Recanting his earlier support for the New Deal—though not for FDR's best lines—he described business leaders as the dam restraining the collective tide, despite the burdens of high taxes, government regulation, and Social Security imposed by liberals. Somehow, his jeremiad sounded upbeat and inspirational rather than a prediction of doom. The message remained nearly constant between the 1950s and the 1980s. General Electric censored his material only once, when he criticized the Tennessee Valley Authority—a major consumer of electrical equipment—as socialistic.

In 1962, General Electric suddenly terminated its association with Reagan. The company had heard rumors of a Justice Department probe into Reagan's activities while SAG president a decade earlier. Allegedly, he had profited from a "sweetheart deal" with the powerful television and film production company, MCA, that allowed it to represent actors as agents while producing shows in which they appeared—an apparent conflict of interest. When called to testify on this charge before a grand jury in 1962, Reagan pled forgetfulness. As president, he often had bouts of memory loss when asked to recall some decision that had gone sour.

Financially secure despite the loss of the GE job, Reagan accepted a few television and film roles. However, he devoted the bulk of his energies between 1962 and 1965 to delivering the speech he had perfected during the previous decade.

The Speech

The evolution of Reagan's conservative thought contrasted with the "mellowing" of mainstream Republican ideology during the 1950s. Although Dwight D. Eisenhower twice trounced the more liberal Democratic presidential nominee Adlai Stevenson, Ike helped lay to rest the pre-New Deal Republican orthodoxy. As he told his brother midway during his presidency, "should any political party attempt to abolish Social Security, unemployment insurance, and eliminate labor laws and farm programs" forged under Roosevelt and Truman, "you would not hear of that party again in our political history."

So-called modern Republicanism, accepting most of the New Deal as a given, antagonized the conservative fringe of the GOP. Loosely known as the "New Right," these dissidents ranged from Robert Welch, who founded the extremist John Birch Society in 1958, to William F. Buckley, who established the respectably conservative journal *National Review* three years earlier. In 1960 Senator Barry Goldwater, Republican of Arizona, published a treatise (ghosted by L. Brent Bozell, Buckley's brother-in-law), *The Conscience of a Conservative*, which became something of a bible to the New Right. Goldwater rejected New Deal social programs, called for the return of laissez-faire capitalism, and urged aggressively challenging the Soviet bloc. The New Right had a strong following in California, the largest state by the mid-1960s, and Reagan focused his speech making there.

In 1964 Barry Goldwater became the White Knight of the conservative movement. Nominated for president by the Republican Party, he promised to dismantle the New Deal legacy at home and abroad. Despite his supporters' hopes, Goldwater proved a divisive and unpopular candidate. President Lyndon B. Johnson portrayed him as an extremist itching to unleash a nuclear war while sending the elderly and infirm to the poorhouse. Late in the faltering campaign, Ronald Reagan offered to make a televised fundraising speech on behalf of the Republican candidate.

The proposed text did not please Goldwater's staff. On paper, it seemed a collection of anti-government, anti-communist cliches that barely mentioned the nominee. But even the conservatives in Goldwater's camp underestimated Reagan's emotional appeal. Brazenly lifting, without attribution, phrases coined by Franklin Roosevelt, Abraham Lincoln, and Winston Churchill, Reagan declared in his October 27, 1964, speech:

> You and I have a rendezvous with destiny. We can preserve for our children this, the last best hope of man on earth, or we can sentence them to take the first step into a thousand years of darkness. If we fail, at least let our children and our children's children, say of us we justified our brief moment here. We did all that could be done.

Reagan laced his address with references to the tax burden and federal debt he described as endangering national survival. Viewers overnight contributed $1 million to the foundering Goldwater campaign.

Columnist David Broder described the performance as the "most successful political debut since William Jennings Bryan electrified the 1896 Democratic Convention with his 'Cross of Gold' speech."

Like Bryan's appeal for silver coinage, Reagan also pitched an economic panacea. He called for the restoration of the supposed message of the nation's "Founding Fathers that outside of its legitimate functions, government does nothing as well or as economically as the private sector of the economy."

Despite Lyndon Johnson's 1964 landslide victory, Republicans found some comfort in election trends. Outside his native Arizona, Goldwater won five states in the deep south by attracting a large number of white Democrats angered by their party's support for civil rights. Republican strategists sensed that working- and middle-class whites, resentful of the aid lavished on "undeserving" minority and poor Americans, could be induced to switch parties at least at the presidential level.

Goldwater proved too abrasive and impatient to capitalize on this phenomenon. But where the senator grimaced and scowled, Reagan smiled and cajoled. His message, though equally conservative, had a self-deprecating and inspirational quality. Within a few months of the Johnson landslide, a group of wealthy Californians, including Homes Tuttle and Henry Salvatori, organized a "Friends of Ronald Reagan" committee to promote his candidacy for governor of California. To their later regret, many Republican and Democratic officials dismissed Reagan as a dilettante.

The 1966 California Election

As in his campaign for the presidency fourteen years later, Ronald Reagan ran for the governorship of California on a promise to reduce the size and scope of state government and to throw the rascals out. "I am not a politician . . . I am an ordinary citizen" opposed to high taxes, government regulation, big spending, waste, and fraud, he declared in 1966. Although he had stressed similar themes in his public speaking since the early 1950s, Reagan was hardly the ingenue he claimed to be. His wealthy backers arranged for political consultant Stuart Spencer, of the firm BASICO, and a team of media specialists to "program" him.

These professionals devised a list of simple issues—and answers—all arranged on easily handled 5×8 index cards for Reagan's reference. The team, in their words, sought to "goof proof" the candidate by limiting his appearances to short presentations in front of friendly audiences with little opportunity for spontaneous questions from the press. Spencer recognized Reagan as a "master of the electronic media" and decided that the candidate's campaign should, as much as possible, be confined to television. Reagan easily won the Republican primary against a weak opponent and went on to challenge the two-term Democratic incumbent, Governor Pat Brown, in the general election.

A moderate Democrat, Brown had presided over a period of rapid growth in California. The state's university and college system, road network, water projects, and social services expanded during Brown's administration, as had taxes. Although the public infrastructure contributed to California's economic success, many middle-class citizens resented rising taxes, the violent Watts ghetto riots of 1965, the Berkeley Free Speech Movement, and the voluble student anti-war movement.

Reagan parlayed these resentments into an effective attack on the incumbent. Instead of detailing his plans for state government, he focused voter attention on symbolic issues, like freedom, personal autonomy, and "traditional values." He linked Brown to big government, high taxes, welfare cheats, ghetto riots, judges who "coddled criminals," and what he called the "mess" at Berkeley. The spoiled "bums," as he called student protestors, indulged in "sexual orgies so vile I cannot describe them to you." Unlike those questioning the Vietnam War, Reagan endorsed General Douglas MacArthur's simple dictum issued during the war in Korea, "there is no substitute for victory." In one particularly strident speech, the candidate proposed to "level Vietnam, pave it, paint stripes on it, and make a parking lot of it." But Reagan typically relied on a more inspirational appeal, telling audiences "We can start a prairie fire that will sweep the nation and prove we are number one in more than crime and taxes . . . this is a dream, as big and golden as California itself."

Reporters covering the 1966 campaign considered Reagan woefully ignorant about state government, yet extremely amiable and cordial on a personal level. When one asked him what kind of governor he would make, he quipped, "I don't know, I've never played a governor." This easy self-parody undercut Pat Brown's effort to portray him as an inflexible ideologue and dangerous extremist. California voters viewed Reagan as a warm and pleasant man aroused by grievances they shared. In the November election Reagan trounced Brown by a margin of nearly a million votes.

Governor Reagan

In January 1967, Ronald Reagan assumed the post of governor in a midnight inauguration, the time selected by Nancy Reagan's astrologer. The Walt Disney Studio designed many of the subsequent festivities. Reagan wrote his own inaugural speech, stating that: "For many years now, you and I have been shushed like children and told there are no simple answers to the complex problems which are beyond our comprehension." The "truth is," he countered, "there are simple answers—there just are not easy ones."

Having won election without a specific agenda, Reagan had difficulty defining his goals. Several months after taking office, he seemed stumped by a reporter's query about his legislative priorities. Turning to an aide he remarked: "I could take some coaching from the sidelines, if anyone can recall my legislative program." For a while he did little more than order across-the-board budget cuts for state agencies, impose a hiring freeze, and request state employees to work without pay on holidays. His cabinet secretary, William Clark, reduced all policy issues to single-page "mini-memos" before the governor read them.

After settling in, Reagan combined conservative rhetoric with fairly flexible policies. Although he several times sent state police to quell disturbances on the Berkeley campus and forced out prominent liberal administrators from the state university system, he ultimately dropped plans to slash education spending and to investigate "communism and blatant sexual misbehavior" at Berkeley. In 1967 he blamed his predecessor for leaving him a budget deficit and then approved the largest tax increase in state history. Although Reagan boasted of cutting expenditures, during his two terms spending doubled, from under $5 billion per year to $10 billion. When the legislature passed one of the nation's most liberal abortion laws, Reagan signed it, later claiming he was not familiar with its provisions and that doctors took advantage of a loophole to perform more abortions than the law intended.

This combination of conservative rhetoric with moderate policy, many believed, represented Reagan's effort to position himself as a presidential candidate in 1968. Richard Nixon, however, secured the nomination that year and again in 1972. Reagan bided his time in Sacramento and won re-election in 1970. During his second administration, Reagan promoted a modest tax reform and led a rhetorical war against "welfare cheats," pledging to help the "tax payer" rather than the "tax taker." The governor and his aides railed against the high cost and moral evil of welfare, but, ultimately, compromised with the Democratic majority in the legislature. The resulting welfare reform bill tightened eligibility standards and anti-fraud measures, included a pilot program requiring some recipients to seek jobs or job training, and raised substantially payments to families. Both conservatives and liberals had something to crow about.

Throughout his eight years as governor, Reagan criticized public programs as inferior to private business, insisting that fiercely independent ranchers and railroad builders had carved an empire from a wild land. He ignored the fact that since the nineteenth century the West, and, especially California, thrived on public water, power, and road projects. As a leading regional historian noted, "the West, more than any other American region, was built by state power, state expertise, state technology, and state bureaucracy."

Presidential Aspirations

In 1973–74, the expanding scandal surrounding the 1972 burglary and cover-up by the Nixon administration of the Democratic National Committee offices at the Watergate building threatened Governor Reagan's political aspirations. Although untainted by Nixon's misdeeds, Reagan had counted on seeking nomination at an open convention in 1976, when he would be 65 years old. If Nixon left office before completing his second term, an appointed successor would have a powerful advantage in securing the nomination. But Nixon's support dissolved in the face of mounting evidence of his wrongdoing and in August 1974 Vice President Gerald

Ford (appointed when Vice President Spiro Agnew resigned after admitting he had taken bribes) replaced Nixon as president.

Reagan's second term as governor ended in January 1975. Although he remained popular, he decided to leave office on a high note rather than seek a third term. He returned to the speaker's circuit, making many live appearances supplemented by radio commentaries and newspaper columns. Energized by these activities, and infuriated by Ford's selection of liberal Republican Nelson Rockefeller as vice president, Reagan resolved to challenge the incumbent for nomination in 1976.

In early primary states, Reagan spoke of a plan to "save" $90 billion by transferring federally funded social programs to the states. When this failed to spark much interest, he attacked President Ford and Secretary of State Henry Kissinger for pursuing arms control and other forms of cooperation with the Soviet Union. Instead of "placating potential adversaries," Reagan called for asserting American power. He particularly condemned negotiations to "give away" the Panama Canal, and charged that Ford had allowed the United States to become "number two in a world where it is dangerous, if not fatal, to be second best."

Reagan won a handful of southern primaries and the California contest, taking his challenge all the way to the nominating convention. But Gerald Ford had enough delegat_s to assure a first ballot victory. He went on to lose the general election to Democrat Jimmy Carter. Some people later speculated that Reagan might have beaten the Georgian in 1976. In fact, polling data indicates that Reagan still lacked a national following and drew most of his strength from southern and western Republicans.

The Carter Hiatus

Undaunted by his near miss, Reagan geared up for the 1980 election soon after Carter took office. He resumed his criticism of Panama Canal negotiations, likening it to a giveaway of the Grand Canyon or Statue of Liberty. But Reagan's argument faltered when two close friends and prominent conservatives, John Wayne and William F. Buckley, were persuaded by Panamanian strongman,

General Omar Torijos, to endorse the treaty that the Senate rati-
fied in April 1978. Thereafter, the issue of the canal quickly faded.

Almost on cue, however, Californians gave Reagan a new platform. In June voters overwhelmingly approved Proposition 13, a
plan to limit local and state property tax. The brain child of 75-
year-old Howard Jarvis, "Prop 13" signified, in its drafter's words,
an effort "to take control of the government again or else it is
going to take control of you." It became shorthand for what *The
New York Times* called a "Primal Scream by the People against
Big Government." Democratic pollster Pat Caddell agreed, telling
President Carter that the vote in California represented a "revolution against government." Opponents of liberalism and the welfare
state used public frustration with taxes to slash revenues as a means
of blocking new programs.

As early as the 1950s, Reagan had criticized high taxes but he
had not made tax reduction a major theme while he governed California. Now, he rushed to find a seat on the anti-tax band wagon.
The passage of Prop 13, he announced, "triggered hope in the breasts
of the people that something could be done . . . a little bit like
dumping those cases of tea off the boat into Boston harbor." Reagan tried to make the movement national by endorsing drastic cuts
in federal income tax rates, an idea already broached by Congressman Jack Kemp and Senator William Roth.

Criticism of government and the taxes that paid for it became
more widespread as the lustre of the Carter administration tarnished. Having won election as an outsider critical of politics-as-
usual, Jimmy Carter lacked natural allies among Democrats or Republicans in Congress. His initial well-meaning but inept effort to
pardon Vietnam draft dodgers and cancel western water projects
of dubious merit alienated powerful figures in both parties. His
tendency to straddle the fence on social issues like abortion and
affirmative action left the impression of moral confusion. Carter
voiced valid concern about the need to devise a responsible energy-
use policy but offered citizens little guidance besides wearing sweaters
and advising them to turn down their thermostats. This led Ronald
Reagan to charge that the energy crisis reflected no "shortage of
oil," only a "surplus of government." Also, inflation grew steeply
after late 1978 when the Iranian revolution (discussed below) drove

the price of oil sharply higher. This tended to discredit still further the half-hearted energy policy.

By July 1979, Carter's approval rate in public opinion polls declined to 29%, almost as low as Nixon's when he resigned. The president's pollster, Pat Caddell, spoke of a "national malaise," which might be shaken off by a political reshuffling. Carter replaced five members of his Cabinet but failed to bolster public confidence in his administration.

Paul Volcker, the newly appointed chairman of the Federal Reserve Board, confronted rising prices, slowed production and mounting unemployment with a plan that drove interest rates above 15% in an effort to stop inflation. Although this proved successful in the long run and was tacitly endorsed by Reagan during the first two years of his own presidency, the policy caused a sharp recession in 1980 and further eroded Carter's popularity.

Despite some significant achievements in foreign policy (including the Panama Canal Treaty and the Camp David Accords making peace between Israel and Egypt), during 1979 and 1980 the Carter administration suffered a series of dramatic rebuffs. At the beginning of his tenure, Jimmy Carter boasted "we are now free of that inordinate fear of communism which once led us to embrace any dictator in that fear." But the Cold War returned with a vengeance when the Soviet Union meddled in the Middle East and Africa. This, along with the Iranian revolution, fatally undermined Carter's claim to foreign affairs leadership.

President Carter also zigzagged between the conflicting advice of Secretary of State Cyrus Vance and National Security Adviser Zbigniew Brzezinski. Vance favored arms control and management of the international economy as a means to reduce conflict and get on with Moscow. Brzezinski advocated power politics and distrusted Soviet motives. It took Vance until June 1979 to achieve a draft arms control treaty with Moscow (SALT II) that limited each side to 2,400 nuclear launchers. By then, however, opponents pointed to Soviet involvement in Africa as proof that the Kremlin retained its expansionist drive.

Concern about Carter's ability to handle foreign affairs increased partly because of the antics of his younger brother, Billy. An irrepressible and somewhat unstable personality, Billy had previously attracted headlines by his flamboyant marketing of "Billy Beer." In 1979 the public learned that Billy had been paid $200,000 to act as an agent of Libya, a nation whose leader, Muammar Qaddafi, was militantly anti-Israel and rumored to support terrorism. When Billy declared that "there are a lot more Arabs than there are Jews," he only made the president's position more uncomfortable.

In December 1979, Soviet forces invaded Afghanistan to protect a dottering communist regime from internal collapse. Many Americans feared this "gravest threat to peace" since 1945, as Carter called it, signalled an impending Soviet drive on the oil-rich Persian Gulf. Carter embargoed grain sales to the Russians, boycotted the upcoming Moscow Olympics, revived draft registration, sped up production of new weapons such as the cruise missile, and withdrew the SALT II treaty from Senate consideration.

Iran and the Crisis of National Confidence

Americans were even more beset by rage and frustration generated by the capture of the American embassy in Teheran on November 4, 1979, and the subsequent captivity of some fifty embassy staff. For over twenty-five years, Iran's ruler, Shah Reza Pahlavi, had been an American client in the Persian Gulf, exercising a moderate influence on oil prices while using his petro-dollars to buy billions of dollars worth of American weapons and products.

Despite some real economic progress in Iran, the Shah's harsh rule and toleration of corruption fueled growing resentment, especially among fundamentalist Muslims who followed an exiled religious leader, the Ayatollah Khomeini. From exile in Iraq and France, Khomeini encouraged a revolution which, in February 1979, drove the Shah from Iran. The following October, when Carter permitted the fatally ill Shah to enter the United States for medical treatment, Khomeini denounced the United States as "the Great Satan" and demanded that Carter turn over the deposed monarch and his alleged foreign wealth to the new Islamic regime. Soon after, a mob sacked the U.S. embassy in Teheran and seized its staff.

At first, Carter's popular standing soared as Americans joined him in denouncing this violation of international law. But as the crisis wore on, the media each night highlighted the number of days (444 before their release) the captives had spent in captivity. Television news broadcasts bearing labels such as "America Held Hostage" made the administration's patience seem like impotence. Gradually, Carter lost control of the situation. Democratic challenger Senator Edward Kennedy complained that Carter could do little more than "lurch from crisis to crisis." Ronald Reagan, by now an announced candidate for the Republican nomination, protested that "our friend" the Shah would still be in power had Carter not criticized him for torturing political prisoners. Carter's inability to free the hostages, Reagan suggested, was just one more sign of his incompetence.

On April 24, 1980, Carter tried to break the deadlock with a rescue mission. Eight helicopters took off from an aircraft carrier in the Persian Gulf, en route for a desert rendezvous with a refueling plane. But one of the choppers suffered an engine failure and the others flew into a dust storm, disabling two. The commander decided that the remaining five could not achieve the rescue and aborted the mission. Then one of the helicopters collided with a refueling plane killing eight servicemen, injuring five, and destroying seven aircraft. In his sorrowful public announcement of the fiasco, Carter spoke of "mechanical failures." But to many Americans the debacle symbolized the unravelling of national power. Some asked if the Three Stooges now directed foreign policy.

The failed rescue mission probably sealed Carter's political fate. Although he managed to beat back Senator Edward Kennedy's challenge to his renomination, he no longer had much credibility. Rather than admiring his credentials as an outsider, many people now ridiculed him as a blunderer. Ronald Reagan turned this crisis of confidence into a successful presidential campaign.

Social-Political Trends and the 1980 Election

Shortly before his death in January 1978, Senator Hubert H. Humphrey restated the foundations of New Deal liberalism. The "moral test of government," the Minnesota Democrat declared, "is how it treats those who are in the dawn of life, the children; those who are in the twilight of life, the aged; and those who are in the shadows of life, the sick, the needy and the handicapped." By such a measure, the liberal agenda still had far to go despite decades of public spending.

Yet critics from the left and right had grown frustrated with the apparent inability of government programs to solve social problems. Business groups charged that government was ill equipped to undertake new initiatives. Many Democrats agreed with Senator Gary Hart, running for re-election in Colorado, who told his constituents: "We are not a bunch of little Hubert Humphreys." California's Democratic governor, Jerry Brown, spoke of a "world with limits to its resources and a country with limits to its power and economy."

The persistence of poverty despite government efforts to alleviate it became a staple criticism among many politicians. Conservatives argued that social and economic problems were actually made worse by liberal remedies. In the late-1970s, Ronald Reagan articulated this thought when he declared "for the average American, the message is clear—liberalism is no longer the answer, it is the problem."

As noted earlier, the "tax revolt" symbolized by the passage of Proposition 13 in 1978 shocked many politicians. Ironically, the effort by Jimmy Carter to reform the federal income tax code by closing many loopholes favoring business and the wealthy fell victim to the anti-tax mood. Wary of being dubbed tax-and-spend liberals, Congressional Democrats approved the Revenue Act of 1978, which closed few loopholes but reduced taxes for the wealthiest 2% of Americans.

The New Right

Since the 1950s, the New Right, or "movement conservatives" as some called themselves in later decades, relished the prospect of sweeping away the network of social programs and regulations enacted since the 1930s. A loose coalition of religious fundamentalists, computerized fund raisers, members of Congress, unorthodox economists, and political action committees put organizational muscle behind the Reagan candidacy.

Whether they had a religious, secular, or congressional background, New Right activists believed that environmentalism, arms control, gun control, abortion rights, gay rights, feminism, welfare, affirmative action, pornography, and the Equal Rights Amendment all fostered a destructive "permissiveness" that undermined the value of family, church, and work.

In the wake of the Watergate scandal, federal laws limited the size of individual and corporate campaign contributions to political candidates. The reform was designed to force political hopefuls to rely on raising small sums from a wider cross section of Americans. Presumably, this would limit the influence of "special interest" groups. The law still allowed small contributions to be amalgamated by so-called Political Action Committees, or PACs, which promoted issues rather than individual candidates. Richard Viguerie, a skilled direct mail fund raiser, developed computerized techniques to track membership lists in "single issue" organizations, such as those opposed to abortion or gun control, and tap these individuals for campaign contributions to specific PACs. He could then connect a local conservative candidate to a large pool of cash controlled by a PAC that endorsed the candidate's platform.

In 1979–80, PACs with a conservative political orientation concentrated their effort on assisting candidates challenging a target list of liberal Democratic senators with national reputations. These included George McGovern of South Dakota, Frank Church of Idaho, John Culver of Iowa, Birch Bayh of Indiana, Warren Magnuson of Washington, Gaylord Nelson of Wisconsin, and Alan Cranston of California.

The New Right's concern with restoring moral order found support among fundamentalist Christian sects. They expressed outrage over the greater acceptance of divorce, abortion, pre-marital sex, homosexuality, and feminism. Jimmy Carter had mobilized fundamentalist Christians in 1976, but Reagan captured the movement four years later. The Christian Right saw most decadent moral trends as the product of "Secular Humanism," their term for a godless, human-centered faith undermining America. Phyllis Schlafly, organizer of the secular Eagle Forum, also appealed to Protestant fundamentalists who maintained that the Bible ordained a woman's submissiveness to her husband, "just as she would submit to Christ as her Lord."

In the decade following 1978, the number of Christian ministries broadcast regularly over television increased from twenty-five to over three hundred. Evangelical Christians carried out a communications revolution. They and Reagan embraced each other, increasing their mutual power throughout the 1980s.

Jerry Falwell, a minister in Virginia, proclaimed that "this country is fed up with radical causes . . . fed up with the unisex movement, fed up with the departure from basics, from decency, from the philosophy of the monogamous home." The free enterprise system, he insisted, "is clearly outlined in the Book of Proverbs." In 1979 Falwell created a political arm of fundamentalism, called the Moral Majority, which sought to arouse evangelical Protestants, to "get them saved, baptized and registered" to vote.

Changes in FCC regulations during the 1970s and 1980s permitted local television stations to sell time to religious broadcasters and count this as fulfilling the stations' public service requirement. By selling airtime to ministers with few scruples about fund raising to pay for the broadcasts, television stations drove off the air clergy who would not solicit money. By 1980, nearly all religion on TV was commercial and most of it was dominated by conservative evangelicals.

Falwell and several other ministers, including Pat Robertson, Jimmy Swaggert, Oral Roberts, and Jim Bakker became especially adept at preaching the gospel on television. By 1980, these so-called Televangelists had a weekly audience estimated at between 60 to 100 million viewers. These electronic ministries combined country music, sermons, and support for conservative causes with an extraordinarily sophisticated fund-raising apparatus.

The Moral Majority and groups like NCPAC (National Conservative Political Action Committee) surveyed local races in 1980 and issued lists of liberals, rated by "moral report cards," to be targeted for defeat. The senators named earlier faced little-known but well-financed opponents able to outspend them. Before the 1980 vote, Senate Democrats held an eighteen-seat majority (fifty-nine to forty-one). The senate that met in January 1981 had a four-seat (fifty-two to forty-eight) Republican majority, the first time the GOP dominated that chamber in nearly three decades.

Although Reagan had a strict religious upbringing, as an adult he seldom attended church and had been divorced. Nevertheless, he embraced the New Right religious movement. During the 1980 campaign he told a convention of fundamentalist Christian leaders that he considered himself "born again" and that "it was a fact that all the [world's] complex and horrendous problems have their answer in that single book—the Bible." He supported calls to teach the biblical account of creation alongside the theory of evolution in public schools and told the cheering ministers, "you can't endorse me, but I endorse you."

In addition to the religious criticism of liberalism, a group of Democrats, called neoconservatives, attacked the direction taken by their party. These intellectuals, several of whom wrote for small but influential journals such as *Commentary* and *The Public Interest,* included Midge Dector, Irving Kristol, Norman Podhoretz, Daniel Bell, Nathan Glazer, and Jeane Kirkpatrick. They accused liberals of distorting the original goals of the welfare state. Government programs that first promoted equal opportunity now sought to guarantee equal results. Policies as varied as affirmative action, detente with the Soviet Union, and social movements like feminism and gay rights particularly offended them as examples of "permissiveness" undermining society.

In 1975 a group of neoconservatives, including the veteran Cold Warrior Paul Nitze, who especially worried about the consequences of Soviet military superiority formed the Committee on the Present Danger. Arguing that detente amounted to unilateral American disarmament and that the Soviet Union had developed the capacity to intimidate if not defeat the United States, they urged the public and Congress to support a large buildup of military power.

Roots of Reaganomics

New Right economic theorists rejected the system of social welfare and business regulation that prevailed since the New Deal. In place of the ideas associated with John Maynard Keynes, so-called supply-siders maintained that a minimalist government that provided few services and levied lower taxes would cure most economic ills. According to this canon, reducing tax rates would promote growth and savings, stimulate commerce, convince people to work harder, reduce inflation, and, incredibly, increase tax revenues.

This idea took specific form in 1974, when an obscure economist from California, Arthur Laffer, drew a graph on a restaurant napkin to demonstrate to a member of President Gerald Ford's staff the possible effects of tax cuts. In a simple drawing, later called the "Laffer Curve," the economist noted the paradox that any tax system would collect inadequate revenues as the rate of taxation approached either 0 or 100%. At the low rate not enough money would come in no matter how much business activity took place. As taxes approached 100%, business activity would cease, limiting revenue collection. Laffer proposed setting tax rates at a point low enough to encourage additional economic activity and thus increase total tax revenues.

It was hard to dispute the principle underlying the graph, but neither Laffer nor his advocates could say what the ideal tax rate ought to be. This made the formula nearly useless. Nevertheless, the idea caught fire among several journalists and politicians who considered it the equivalent of the mythical Philosopher's Stone, a device for turning lead into gold. Among Laffer's principal disciples was Jude Wanniski, an editorial writer for the *Wall Street Journal.* He promoted Laffer's ideas in his newspaper and organized a like-minded group called "the cabal." In 1978, these activists persuaded two Republicans, Congressman Jack Kemp of New York and Senator William Roth of Delaware, to introduce legislation that proposed a 30% reduction in federal income taxes. Kemp predicted this action would quickly free the "creative genius that has always invigorated America" but lay "submerged, waiting like a genie in a bottle to be loosed."

In 1980 Ronald Reagan conferred with Laffer, Kemp, and Wanniski who, in the words of then Michigan congressman and later head of the Office of Management and Budget, David Stockman, "thoroughly hosed him down with supply-side doctrine." Wanniski reported that the Laffer Curve "set off a symphony" in Reagan's ears. He knew "instantly that it was true and would never have a doubt thereafter."

In fact, doubt remains whether Reagan either understood or believed the grand claims of Laffer and Wanniski. During the presidential campaign, Stockman was assigned to prepare Reagan for his debate with Jimmy Carter. Stockman believed that Reagan "had only the foggiest idea of what supply side was all about." In fact, Stockman later wrote, supply-side doctrine "was always a Trojan Horse," a euphemism for the old "trickle-down" theory that cutting taxes for business and the wealthy would stimulate the economy.

Even before Reagan's election, Stockman suspected that a major tax cut, unless accompanied by massive reductions in spending, would produce budget deficits surpassing $100 billion per year. Since Reagan promised to increase military spending and balance the budget, the new administration would have to drastically cut domestic spending. Stockman actually saw this as a clever strategy to implement a "blueprint for sweeping, wrenching change in national economic governance." Supply-side policies would not have much effect on the economy, Stockman surmised, but might compel Congress to slash social welfare spending as a response to a swelling deficit. Reagan himself never admitted such a motive.

The Election of 1980

Ronald Reagan formally declared his presidential candidacy in November 1979. As the oldest of ten Republicans in the race, and someone already rejected by his party, the press did not take him very seriously. Journalists who listened to his announcement dismissed it as a cliched attack on big government. But once again, they misjudged Reagan's effective use of television. He discussed his humble origins, his career as an actor, soldier, and union official, his background as a Democrat, and his move to the Republican Party. The candidate recounted his family's hardship during the Depression and how his father had lost his job on Christmas Eve. As his eyes grew visibly moist before the cameras, Reagan declared: "I cannot and will not stand by while inflation and joblessness destroy the dignity of our people."

George Bush, a former Congressman from Texas, Republican Party chairman, and CIA director under President Ford, gave Reagan the greatest challenge. He dubbed the tax-cut plan and Laffer curve "voodoo economics," while Reagan called Bush too liberal on abortion, gun control, and women's rights. Bush narrowly won the Iowa caucuses, but Reagan beat him in the New Hampshire primary in February 1980 and dominated the rest of the campaign. At the party nominating convention that summer, Reagan easily took a first ballot victory.

In a move to assuage Republican moderates, the nominee toyed with the idea of asking Gerald Ford to serve as his running mate. The former president would have special responsibility for foreign affairs. But this awkward idea fell flat. Instead, Reagan reached out to his main opponent, George Bush, to run as the vice-presidential nominee.

Reagan left the convention with a centrist running mate, a unified party behind him, and a large lead in the opinion polls. He faced, veteran journalist Lou Cannon observed, a Democratic incumbent "dogged by the captivity of hostages he could not free, an economy he could not seem to improve, a brother he could not disown, and an opponent he could not shake." In retrospect, the most surprising thing about the 1980 campaign was how narrowly Reagan avoided losing to someone so unpopular.

During the fall, Reagan made a series of gaffes that his handlers labored to cover up. While travelling to speak to delegates of the National Urban League, his only speech to a predominantly African-American group during the campaign, Reagan stopped off at the Neshoba County fair in Philadelphia, Mississippi, close by where three civil rights workers had been murdered in 1964. Congressmen Trent Lott had invited him and Reagan rejected appeals by his staff to cancel the appearance. He explained that as an actor he learned never to cancel a performance once his billing had been announced. (This stubborn streak caused him grief five years later when he insisted on speaking at a German cemetery after it became known that Nazi SS troops were interred there.) At the fair, he declared he "believed in states' rights" and promised to restore to local and state governments "the powers which properly belonged to them."

Speaking to the Veterans of Foreign Wars in August, Reagan wrote a passage into his prepared speech in which he blamed past administrations for not fighting for victory in Vietnam. Rubbing salt in a wound, the candidate declared "it is time we recognize that ours, in truth, was a noble cause." Reagan attacked Carter for establishing diplomatic ties with China and implied that, once elected, he would restore recognition of Taiwan.

At a convention of Christian fundamentalists that same month, Reagan shared the platform with a speaker who declared "God doesn't hear the prayers of a Jew." The candidate declared himself "born again," as well as a believer in the literal interpretation of the Bible. Creationism, he explained, should be taught in public schools as an alternative to theories of evolution. A Reagan aide rued that the candidate made "so many blunders, reporters had to pick and choose which ones they would write about."

To correct this problem as well as other pitfalls of the campaign, Reagan's staff brought back Stuart Spencer, the consultant who "goof proofed" the candidate in 1966. Spencer persuaded Reagan to stop giving unrehearsed answers to reporters' questions. The staff would prepare answers in advance for him to give whatever the question. This stabilized the campaign, although Reagan fell off the wagon at least one more time when he declared that trees, not industry or cars, caused most air pollution. The next day, during a Reagan speech at Claremont College, students hung signs on trees which read "chop me down before I kill again."

Partly because of such gaffes, Jimmy Carter believed he could demolish Reagan's candidacy in a one-on-one debate. (Carter refused to acknowledge third-party candidate John Anderson.) Like Pat Brown in 1966 and Bush during the earlier primaries, Carter thought Reagan would come across to voters as a foolish amateur unable to hold his own against a withering barrage of facts and figures.

Carter's optimism had some basis in fact, since opinion polls through late October showed him trailing the challenger by only a few points. Reagan's team greatly feared that a last-minute release of the Americans held hostage in Iran might yet salvage Carter's presidency. In August, according to Reagan's close adviser Michael Deaver, the staff predicted Carter might orchestrate an "October

Reagan confers with campaign manager and later CIA Director William J. Casey during the 1980 campaign. *Courtesy AP/Wide World Photos.*

surprise," the freeing of the captives on election eve. Public euphoria, Deaver believed, would have "rolled over the land like a tidal wave. Carter would have been a hero," the complaints against him forgotten. "He would have won."

Deaver's mention of the anxiety felt in the Reagan campaign coincides with rumors that persisted for a decade that someone close to Reagan, perhaps campaign director William Casey, cut a secret deal with Iran before the 1980 election. Allegedly, Casey met with Iranian representatives in Madrid during October 1980 and urged that the American hostages *not* be released before the November election. In return, the new administration would indirectly or directly resume military sales to Iran, whose armed forces desperately required U.S. replacement parts.

Some circumstantial evidence supports these allegations. For example, during August and September, Carter's aides had made progress in negotiations with Iran and expected an imminent hostage release. Suddenly, however, the Iranians broke off talks. Carter and CIA director Admiral Stansfield Turner soon learned that Israel had shipped critical U.S.-licensed military equipment to Iran, alleviating some of the pressure on Teheran. Israel, like Iran, many officials suspected, hoped to fare better under a new president. William Casey, some evidence suggests, introduced his Iranian contacts to Israelis during the summer of 1980.

Ronald Reagan's campaign behavior also raises an intriguing question. Despite his general criticism of Carter, he refrained from vigorously attacking the incumbent's handling of the hostage issue until October 20, 1980, when he declared "I don't know why fifty-two Americans have been held hostage for almost a year now." He promised, if elected, to strengthen the CIA and other agencies to punish terrorists. Significantly, October 20 is the date offered for Casey's supposed deal with Iran to hold the hostages until after the November 4 election.

Then CIA Director Turner knew that three Reagan aides, Laurence H. Silberman, Richard V. Allen, and Robert C. McFarlane met at least once with a representative of Khomeini in Washington. (McFarlane later became the president's National Security Adviser and played a key role in the Iran-Contra affair.) They insisted, however, that no bargains were struck and that no further meetings took place. As late as 1991, Turner accepted this version, even writing in his memoir *Terrorism and Democracy* (1991) that any allegation that Reagan or his aides made a deal was "so callous that I find it hard to believe."

For Turner, like many others who had put aside their suspicion, events in the spring of 1991 rekindled their curiosity. In April historian and former Carter administration Iran specialist, Gary Sick, presented new evidence in an article published in *The New York Times*. Sick, who initially doubted the existence of a secret deal, had interviewed separately a dozen or more Iranian arms dealers and intelligence operatives who confirmed in some detail the outlines of a secret approach orchestrated by Casey. Even allowing for the mixed motives of the informants, their stories were compelling and several were able to prove they were in Madrid on the dates in question. Casey, who died in 1987, could not tell his side of the story. However, the Reagan campaign director appears to have dropped out of sight during the key October 1980 days and his whereabouts remain something of a mystery.

Reagan declined to respond formally to any of these charges. Reporters prodded a statement from him on June 15, 1991, while he played golf in California with his successor, George Bush. Dismissing Sick's contention as "absolute fiction," Reagan then admitted that he "did some things to try the other way . . . to get them [the hostages] home." He refused to say more, insisting that some of these "things" were "classified." What "things" private citizen Ronald Reagan might have done in 1980 that had to remain classified eleven years later were anybody's guess. In fact, not only good taste but federal law (the Logan Act) barred private citizens from engaging in negotiations with foreign powers. No one involved in the authorized negotiations knew what he was talking about.

Even if, at Reagan's behest or on his own, Casey had urged the Iranians to speed a hostage release, the mere fact of his opening a second, secret negotiating channel might have prompted the Iranians to raise their demands. As Sick and others remarked, an old Persian saying holds "it's better to have two bidders for your rug than one bidder." Still, during the 1980 campaign, the public knew nothing of these possible events.[1]

When the candidates debated in Cleveland on October 28, Carter spoke of how well the public had responded to hardship. "We have demanded the American people sacrifice, and they have done that very well." Reagan retorted simply, "we do not have to go on sharing in sacrifice." Disputing how Carter criticized his stand on Medicare, Reagan made the audience laugh by saying "there you go again," the tag line of an old film. When Carter said he discussed the dangers of war with his young daughter Amy, Reagan (and many Americans) wondered if he meant Amy was his nuclear arms adviser.

Reagan's skill and training as an actor helped him immeasurably.

---

[1] As a result of Gary Sick's work, later expanded in a book, *October Surprise* (1991), Stansfield Turner and other Carter-era officials changed their views about the possibility of a secret deal with Iran. In 1991, Congress initiated a preliminary investigation of the charges.

By standing tall, speaking clearly, and looking comfortable before the camera, Reagan became an acceptable alternative to someone who had lost favor with the electorate. In his summary statement at the end of the debate, he focused his cheerful blue eyes on the camera and urged Americans to ask themselves "the basic question of our lives: Are you happier today than when Mr. Carter became president of the United States?" Simply by coming across as avuncular and warm, rather than a mad bomber, Reagan had to be judged the "winner."

Over the next few days, as the prospect of a hostage release faded and the results of the debate hit home, Carter's support collapsed. Nearly 40% of perspective voters told pollsters they favored the challenger simply because he was not Carter. Whatever Reagan did, many Americans felt, would be better than the hand wringing, sermons, and demands for sacrifice of the last four years. When the polls closed on November 4, 1980, Reagan had won a slight majority (51%) of the popular vote, a resounding victory (489 to 49) in the electoral college, and helped elect eleven additional Republican senators and nearly three dozen new Republican representatives on his coattails.[2]

Only 11% of those who voted for Reagan in 1980 indicated they preferred him because "he is a real conservative." Most told pollsters they simply felt "it's time for a change." Choosing Reagan represented more a rejection of a failed incumbent and the disaffiliation of voters from the Democratic Party than the formation of a new conservative consensus. In any case, the long-retired actor was about to play the most important role of his lifetime.

[2] Carter received 41% of the popular vote and third-party candidate John Anderson took 7%. Reagan's greatest support came from white males under age 35 who liked his promise to stand up to the Soviet Union. Women of all ages and voters over age 65, more concerned about social programs, provided less support, creating what analysts called the age and gender gaps. During the 1980s, leaders of both parties debated the significance of these gaps. Democrats seemed unsure whether they would increase voter appeal by tailoring their message more to "macho" young men or to women and the elderly. Republicans asked themselves the same question, but faced less of a dilemma since they captured a majority of presidential voters.

2

The Domestic Achievement, 1981–1989

D URING HIS eight years as president, Ronald Reagan challenged many and reversed some of the liberal programs that dominated the federal government since the New Deal. His administration worked to roll back the network of social welfare programs, limit the role of federal courts in promoting civil rights and liberties, eliminate government regulation of business, banking, and the environment, reduce federal taxes, and foster a conservative social ethic regarding reproductive rights, the role of religion in public life, and drug use. The president and his aides believed that by removing the dead hand of government regulation from the private sector, they would unleash market forces, create new wealth, and foster greater equality.

Scoffing at those who spoke of a national "malaise," Reagan's inaugural speech proclaimed "it is time for us to realize that we are too great a nation to limit ourselves to small dreams." Past policies of tax and spend had led to "mortgaging our future and our children's future." The nation must "stop living beyond our means" or face disaster. The new president pledged to cut taxes and end deficit spending. "To paraphrase Winston Churchill," he added, "I did not take the oath I've just taken with the intention of presiding over the dissolution of the world's strongest economy." The American people, tired of calls to reconcile themselves to limits in a world where their nation's power had slipped, generally cheered this promise to restore glory.

Ronald Reagan's favorite speechwriter, Peggy Noonan, sensing the president's desire to "cheer everyone up," drafted many of his best received lines, such as those for the 1984 campaign. "America is back," she wrote, it's "morning again." College students liked talk of renewal from America's oldest serving president. On campuses, where a few years before undergraduates had pelted Lyndon Johnson and Richard Nixon, 20-year-olds screamed "U.S.A! U.S.A!" in response to Reagan's oratory. He tapped a popular yearning to restore a sense of community, real or imagined, lost over the previous two decades. Speaking of the 1984 election, White House Assistant Chief of Staff, Michael Deaver, boasted "we kept apple pie and the flag going the whole time." In many ways, Deaver's comments applied to Reagan's entire presidency.

Wake Up Call

At 7 A.M. on January 20, 1981—inauguration day—Jimmy Carter placed a call from the Oval Office to president-elect Reagan, then at Blair House, the official guest residence across the street. Bone weary after two days with scarcely any sleep, Carter wanted to inform his imminent successor that a plane now waited on the runway in Teheran, scheduled at long last to carry the American captives to freedom. After months of dashed hopes and aborted deals, the powerholders in Iran finally agreed to release the hostages in return for a pledge to arbitrate the unfreezing of Iranian assets in Western banks. Reagan's staff took Carter's call, explaining that the president-elect was sleeping soundly "and was not to be disturbed." Jimmy Carter could hardly believe he would not want to hear the hopeful news. But the president was put off with the promise that when Reagan awoke, if he were interested, he "may call back later."

Reagan's staff knew his instincts. Shortly before the election he snapped at a campaign aide who awakened him earlier than was his custom. "You'd better get used to it, governor," Stuart Spencer explained. "When you're president, that fellow from the National

Security Council will be there to brief you at 7:30 every morning." Then "he's going to have a helluva long wait," Reagan growled. After January 20, 1981, the NSC briefings began at 9:30 A.M.

Carter paced and prayed all morning on inauguration day, anxious for word of the hostage release. He barely took time to shave and dress for the noontime swearing-in of his successor. When the limousine carrying the president-elect arrived at the White House en route to the Capital Hill ceremony, Reagan, in an aside to Michael Deaver, asked, "Did you get a look at Carter?" Unaware of what the incumbent had gone through, Reagan expressed shock at Carter's gaunt appearance. The Iranians, in a final jab at Carter, waited until 12:35 P.M., minutes after Reagan had taken the oath of office as the fortieth President of the United States, to allow the plane to take off. By then, Reagan's staff had begun redecorating the White House. Attuned to their chief's political preferences, they removed a portrait of Harry S Truman from the Cabinet Room and replaced it with one of Calvin Coolidge, perhaps best remembered for his aphorism, "the business of America is business."

Reagan looked marvelous on inauguration day, as if born to wear the formal morning suit he selected for the oath taking. As a result of his acting experience, the new president had an unerring sense that the American people took pleasure in seeing their leaders glamorously attired and slightly above the fray. As he told David Brinkley near the end of his presidency, "there have been times in this office when I've wondered how you could do the job if you hadn't been an actor."

In the evening, following the inauguration, Ronald and First Lady Nancy Reagan, dressed impeccably in tuxedo and designer gown, hosted a round of fancy balls. It was, as one of the party planners remarked, intended as a celebration of "class and dignity" after the dreariness of the previous administration. Where Jimmy Carter had casually strolled down Pennsylvania Avenue, worn sweaters when addressing a television audience, urged Americans to lower their thermostats, and carried his own suitcase, the Reagan era began with glittering celebrations that seemed modeled on parties featured on the television show "Lifestyles of the Rich and Famous." Transportation was strictly via stretch limousine. Although it cost

Reagan at work in the White House. *Courtesy U.S. National Archives.*

$2,000 to rent a luxury vehicle for the four days of festivities, they were in such demand that cars were hired from as far away as Atlanta and New York.

The New Team

The new president made nods toward his most conservative back-ers but seldom selected them for influential positions in his admin-istration. Reagan reached beyond the New Right to appoint many moderate Republicans who had served Presidents Ford and Nixon. In an especially astute move, he appointed James A. Baker, III, a close friend of Vice President George Bush, as White House Chief of Staff, even though this meant disappointing Edwin Meese who expected the job. Unlike Meese, who often got bogged down in details and provoked fights with political opponents, Baker proved exceptionally skilled at moving legislation through Congress. He seemed to recall Lyndon Johnson's remark after the Democrat's landslide victory in 1964. It did not matter how big the margin of victory, Johnson observed, you still had "only one year when

Congress treats you right, then they start worrying about themselves."

Baker argued that key legislation must be passed in the first year of the Reagan administration, while the Democrats in both houses remained in shock and the new Republican majority in the Senate was eager to lead. The chief of staff persuaded Reagan to emphasize two items: tax cuts and the defense buildup. "If we can do that," Baker predicted, "the rest [of the agenda] will take care of itself."

Baker did not mind Reagan's continued calls for banning abortion, permitting school prayer, and amending the constitution to mandate a balanced budget—so long as he did not expend much political capital in pressing Congress to act on these controversial measures. The president's inner feelings about Baker's strategy are hard to fathom, since all he said when presented with the administration's game plan was "sounds great."

The most important individuals in the first administration had authority by virtue of their relationship with Reagan, not their nominal position. Besides Baker, two close associates from Reagan's days as governor held key White House jobs. Meese served as Counselor, a somewhat amorphous post but one that provided regular access to Reagan. Assistant Chief of Staff Michael Deaver was a skilled public relations expert and exceptionally close to both Reagans, who considered him a surrogate son. Deaver arranged the bulk of the president's schedule, controlled media access to him, and had the task of implementing suggestions made to Nancy Reagan by astrologers she consulted. Deaver's intimacy with the First Family prompted one jealous staffer, Patrick Buchanan, to dub him "Lord of the Chamber Pot." In any case, the triumvirate of Baker, Meese, and Deaver played a major role in the success of Reagan's first term.

Among the Cabinet, only those who Reagan either knew before or took a personal liking to played much of a role in governing. Caspar Weinberger, a veteran of both the Nixon administration and Governor Reagan's cabinet, became a powerful force as Secretary of Defense. David Stockman, an effective advocate of Reagan's economic agenda, wielded great influence as Director of the Office of Management and Budget. CIA director William Casey also had the President's ear and, it developed, near blanket authority to run covert operations. Attorneys General William French Smith and, later, Ed Meese, also traced their influence in the Justice Department back to service in Sacramento. Treasury Secretary Donald Regan only occasionally discussed economic policy with the President but still formed a strong bond with hi⋯. Reagan was intrigued by the similarity of their surnames and especially liked Regan's generous supply of off-color "locker room" humor.

Jokes and anecdotes played an unusually important role in the administration pecking order. Probably from his long experience of performing in public, Reagan appreciated humor, human interest stories, and unusual statistics as a way of forging an emotional bond with and, in a way, emotional distance and control over, his audience. Insiders knew that the surest way to endear themselves to the boss was to ply him with jokes and stories he could add to his own repertoire. Donald Regan, who some thought must have hired a gag writer on the Treasury Department payroll, sensed this at once. In contrast, neither Secretary of State Alexander Haig nor United Nation's Ambassador Jeane Kirkpatrick ever mastered the trick of humoring the President. Although both articulated a tough foreign policy that Reagan admired, neither gained admission to his inner circle. Haig lasted barely 18 months before the White House announced his resignation. Kirkpatrick stayed longer but never wielded much influence.

President Reagan made a public display of relying heavily on his Cabinet in forming and implementing policy. In fact, it played a minor role. As even Michael Deaver admitted in 1984, the president often napped during Cabinet discussions because they were boring and irrelevant. This was hardly surprising since Reagan barely knew or cared about many of the people he named to Cabinet posts. He virtually ignored the Departments of Health and Human Services, Commerce, Transportation, Energy, Interior, Education, and Housing and Urban Development. Most of these departments experienced major cuts in budget and personnel between 1981–89. Except for Secretary of the Interior James Watt and Energy Secretary James Edwards (neither of whom lasted through the first administration), the New Right had few representatives in the Cabinet.

Reagan and Vice President Bush. *Courtesy U.S. National Archives.*

In the summer of 1981, movement conservatives felt especially betrayed when Reagan nominated Arizona judge Sandra Day O'Connor to replace retiring Supreme Court Justice Potter Stewart. The right wing considered her insufficiently anti-abortion and wanted a more active judicial conservative to replace the moderate Stewart. Moral Majority leader, the Reverend Jerry Falwell, urged "all good Christians" to oppose her confirmation. The dispute passed only when Senator Barry Goldwater, godfather of the New Right and a supporter of fellow Arizonan O'Connor, declared "every good Christian ought to kick Jerry Falwell right in the ass."

Economic Agendas

Since the 1950s, Reagan had criticized high taxes and the government spending they paid for. As president, he was determined to do something about it. A wealthy man since 1945, he resented the progressive income tax and told anecdotes about how high tax rates discouraged actors from working harder. His point of reference was the early 1950s when his income placed him in the 90% bracket.

Reagan recalled that "you could only make four pictures [a year] and then you were in the top bracket." So instead of working more, "we all quit after four pictures and went off to the country."

Aside from the fact that many taxpayers in the top bracket enjoyed generous "loopholes," the very concept of progressive taxation offended Reagan. Ever since the momentum provided by passage of Proposition 13, his public statements stressed that people should be rewarded for achieving wealth, not taxed at higher rates for doing so. While the hard-working middle class and rich were being soaked, he lambasted the fabled "welfare queens" who drove Cadillacs and had their snoots in the public trough. The rich, Reagan seemed to argue, would not work harder because they did not get to keep enough money; the poor did not work harder because they received too much.

In February 1981, President Reagan unveiled his economic plan before a joint session of Congress. (The full proposal bore the title "America's New Beginning: A Program for Economic Recovery.") "Can we who man the ship of state," he asked rhetorically, "deny that it is somewhat out of control?" Without dwelling on particulars, he described "waste and fraud in the federal government" as a "national scandal." As the nation's debt approached a trillion dollars, did the Democrats believe "we can continue on the present course without coming to a day of reckoning?"

The president's tax initiative (derived from the Kemp-Roth plan) would cut federal income and business tax rates by 30% over three years, eliminate "bracket creep" (the inflationary calculation that pushed taxpayers into higher brackets), reduce taxes on capital gains, lower estate and gift taxes, and allow faster depreciation on business investments.

On the expenditure side of the equation, Reagan sought to cut the inherited Carter budget by $41 billion and to shift many social programs to the states. His spending plan would eliminate numerous welfare programs, trim Social Security, and cut back on parts of the federal bureaucracy that regulated business, the environment, and public health.

The president's chief economic lobbyists, Treasury Secretary Donald Regan and Office of Management and Budget Director David Stockman, told Congress that the spending and tax cuts would together assure prosperity. They claimed business investment would rise 11% a year above inflation and spending on new plants and equipment would rise to 12% of GNP. Most economists gasped in disbelief, since the peacetime American economy had never produced such rates of investment.

Although some critics later described Reagan as lazy, no one could accuse him of not pressing for passage of his economic and defense programs. During his first four months in office, he met with members of Congress about 70 times to lobby for the combination of tax and budget cuts and the military buildup. He appealed frequently to the public and made special effort to court conservative Southern Democrats, the so-called Boll Weevils, in the House.

Reagan even turned near tragedy into a powerful force assisting his program. Just nine weeks into his first term, on March 30, 1981, a crazed gunmen, John Hinckley, shot the president. Hinckley suffered from the delusion that political assassination would win the affections of actress Jodie Foster, a star in the film *Taxi Driver* whose plot included the attempted murder of a politician. Hinckley, firing a cheap handgun loaded with exploding bullets, hit Reagan an inch from the heart and gravely wounded several bystanders, including presidential press secretary James Brady.

In the hospital emergency room, the president told his wife, who looked at him with her usual adoring eyes, "Honey, I forgot to duck." Some older Americans probably recognized these as the words spoken by boxer Jack Dempsey after losing a bout to Gene Tunney in the 1920s. About to go under the surgeon's knife, Reagan jokingly asked if the surgical staff were Republicans. "We're all Republicans today," came the reply. During his recovery, Reagan observed that "God must have been sitting on his shoulder." Whatever "time I've got left," he announced solemnly, "belongs to someone else." This spunk, as well as the president's surprisingly rapid recovery, evoked optimism and appreciation among Americans. Eager to suspend judgment and wish him well, the public and Congress increased their support for his initiatives. By the summer of 1981, the public favored passage of the administration's economic program by a margin of two to one.

Reagan appeared a decisive and successful leader in other ways early in his administration. In August 1981, four months after the attempt of his life, almost 12,000 unionized air traffic controllers violated a no-strike clause in their contract and walked off the job. The Professional Air Traffic Controllers Organization (PATCO), which endorsed Reagan's candidacy, had legitimate complaints about the difficult job performed by the understaffed controllers and thought the president would tacitly accept their job action.

They guessed wrong. Despite his own stint as president of the Screen Actors Guild, Reagan had little sympathy with labor unions and relished the opportunity to impress Congress and the public with his decisiveness. The president warned striking controllers to honor their contract or face dismissal. When the deadline for compliance lapsed, Reagan promptly fired them and ordered military personnel into airport towers to keep commercial aviation flying.

As Reagan supposed, the public admired his tough stand and blamed the controllers, not him, for ensuing air traffic delays. PATCO's arrogance and bloated demands for salary raises alienated many potential sympathizers. By breaking the strike, Reagan intimidated the labor movement and moderated future wage hikes. More important, he enhanced his image of decisiveness. *Washington Post* reporter Haynes Johnson noted that foreign financiers often mentioned that they decided to invest more money in the United States "when Reagan broke the controllers' strike."

Taxes and Deficits

The tax cut passed by Congress on July 29, 1981, reduced federal rates by 5%–10%–10% over three years, slightly below the originally proposed 30%. It was something of a grab bag of favors, benefiting the wealthy and business disproportionately. Overall, its greatest impact was to shift priorities toward military spending and away from social programs.

From the beginning, Budget Director David Stockman told his colleagues that without "draconian reduction on the expenditure side," staggering budget deficits would result from Reagan's tax cut. As a relatively recent convert to the idea of laissez-faire capitalism, Stockman had discarded earlier belief in fundamentalist Christianity and Marxism. Privately, he expected that a rising deficit would force a "politically painful shrinkage of the American welfare state." By slashing Social Security, Medicare, Veterans Hospitals, public housing grants, farm subsidies, public broadcasting, and student loans, Stockman hoped to create a "minimalist government . . . a spare and stingy creature which offered even-handed public justice but no more."

Both Stockman and Treasury Secretary Donald Regan supposed that the president wanted to cut spending heavily, but never really discussed the subject with him. Regan usually gauged the president's views by "studying his speeches and reading the newspapers." Stockman often discussed tactics with Reagan, especially how to buy off with special legislative favors members of Congress wavering in their support of the administration's tax and spending cuts. But the two men never shared their respective visions of the nation's economic future.

As it happened, neither Congress nor the president were prepared to cut deeply into many of the programs on Stockman's hit list. These so-called entitlements, like Medicare and Social Security, constituted 48% (in 1982) of the federal budget. Defense accounted for about 25% and debt service for 10%. Reagan intended to boost defense spending and could not stop paying interest on the debt. Entitlements benefited working- and middle-class Americans, not just the poor and minorities. This meant that about 85% of the federal budget was practically politically untouchable. To avoid a huge deficit, budget reductions of several hundred billion dollars per year would have to come from popular entitlements, from the vulnerable 15% of the budget—or not at all.

For many years, Reagan had criticized Social Security as both an infringement on freedom and a bad economic bargain, since workers, living longer, took more out of the system than they contributed. By the early 1980s, Social Security accounted for 21% of total federal spending. Some bipartisan support existed in 1981 to gradually rein in Social Security costs. David Stockman preferred a more radical proposal slashing benefits, especially for those retiring before age 65.

When Congress soundly rejected this, Reagan appointed a bipartisan commission that unveiled a plan following the 1982 election to raise payroll taxes and limit some cost increases. This promised to keep Social Security viable and eliminate it as a political issue. Whatever the merits of the solution, the episode convinced David Stockman that Reagan had no "blueprint for radical governance." Like Congress, he preferred to cut taxes deeply and spending slightly, lest he squander political good will. Columnist George Will, more perceptive than Stockman, understood the context in which Reagan and Congress acted. "Americans are conservative," Will noted. "What they want to conserve is the New Deal."

The Democratic majority in the House did limit the assault on social welfare spending first proposed by Reagan. But as strongly as the public wanted to preserve Social Security, they wanted taxes reduced. Even though many members of Congress, including Republicans, privately doubted the President's claim that large tax reductions would cause an economic surge that would make up for the lost revenue, the House and Senate approved the 25% tax reductions along with modest reductions in social spending. The axe fell most heavily on the remnants of Great Society programs that helped the poor.

Aside from its impact on people, the most telling result was a staggering rise in the deficit, just as David Stockman predicted in 1981. Reagan took office bitterly critical of Carter's "runaway deficit of nearly $80 billion" and the cumulative national debt of $908 billion. He relished describing how a stack of dollars as tall as the debt would stretch into space. Over the next eight years, however, his administration ran up annual deficits that ranged from a "low" of $128 billion to well over $200 billion. The national debt nearly tripled, to almost $2.7 trillion, by 1989. The Treasury had to borrow about $5,000 for each American, making the $200 billion per year debt service the third largest item in the federal budget.

Several times during the first administration, Stockman tried to engage the president in a discussion of the deficit and the need to curb spending and raise taxes. At these times, the Budget Director recalled, Reagan stopped listening. Instead he "ignored all the palpable, relevant facts and wandered in circles." Reagan blamed runaway spending on an "iron triangle" of Congress, special interest lobbyists, and journalists who allegedly orchestrated a raid on the Treasury. He neglected to mention that he never submitted a balanced budget to Congress. Nor did Congress initiate many new programs during his eight years in office. Most of the red ink resulted from the revenue shortfall caused by lower tax rates combined with increased defense spending, not new social spending.

When the deficit Stockman warned of arrived in 1982, Reagan blamed it on Jimmy Carter and insisted the Treasury would soon have a surplus that would allow him to "start retiring the national debt." By 1984, however, the president described his earlier promise to balance the budget by that year as only a "goal." He continued to urge passage of a constitutional amendment mandating a balanced budget, but insisted it apply to his successors. Pressed by the administration, Congress passed in mid-decade the Gramm-Rudman-Hollings Act, which committed the legislative and executive branches to move toward a balanced budget within a few years. However, it placed many popular big ticket items "off budget" and had little effect.

Although the president publicly rebuffed advice from some of his advisers that he raise taxes to stem the rising tide of red ink, he quietly approved "revenue enhancements." In 1982, 1983, and 1984, Congress voted and Reagan signed legislation increasing "sin" taxes levied on alcohol and tobacco. "User fees" were raised on a variety of federal services. Most important, the payroll tax funding Social Security rose. Because of this and various state tax increases, the total tax bite for the average American family hardly changed during the 1980s, despite the hoopla of federal tax cuts.

On the average, during the 1980s government borrowing to finance deficits absorbed three-quarters of the net savings of all American families and business. Despite predictions, Reagan's policies failed to increase personal or business savings. The rate actually decreased to 5.7% from the 8% level of the Carter years. As a result, more savings went toward financing the deficit and fewer dollars were available for investment in research, new plants, and machinery. America's factories declined relative to those in other countries, contributing to a long-term loss of competitiveness.

GI Joe

"Defense is not a budget item," Ronald Reagan told his staff, "you spend what you need." And spend they did. Defense Secretary

Caspar Weinberger had worked for Nixon and for Governor Reagan. He took office convinced that the United States had unilaterally disarmed itself for a decade, in spite of a relentless Soviet arms buildup. Weinberger fancied himself an amateur historian and believed that America's position in 1981, in relation to the Soviet Union, was equivalent to Britain's in the 1930s in relation to the Nazis. His hero, Winston Churchill, had saved Britain through rearmament. The Defense Secretary considered it vital to assist Churchill's American equivalent (Ronald Reagan) to save his nation in time of peril. The Defense Secretary hung a plaque behind his desk that contained an aphorism spoken by Churchill: "Never give in, never give in, never, never, never; in anything great or small, large or petty, never give in."

Weinberger proposed annual defense spending increases about 10% above the last Carter budget. Compounded over five years, this totaled almost $1.5 trillion through 1986. Not only was this much higher than Reagan had promised during his campaign, but due to a mathematical error discovered belatedly by Budget Director David Stockman, planners arrived at this figure by mistake. The correct five-year total, Stockman realized, should be about $200 billion less. Weinberger reacted furiously when Stockman pointed out the error and sought permission to trim slightly the larger than intended defense buildup. Refusing to "give in," the Defense Secretary complained that even tiny reductions would increase the risk of war.

Unable to settle the matter between themselves, Stockman and Weinberger appealed to the president during a White House conference. The Defense Secretary described "how awesome the Soviets were and how far behind we were." Anyone taking a nickel from the proposed budget, he implied, "wanted to keep us behind the Russians." Weinberger brought charts superimposing Soviet defense plants on a map of Washington. Other illustrations and graphs depicted Soviet nuclear and conventional forces dwarfing those of the free world. "Sir, our B-52 planes are older than their pilots," the Secretary declared while the president nodded in agreement.

As Stockman watched in shock, Weinberger also presented a blow-up cartoon in the form of a poster depicting three soldiers. One was a pygmy who carried no rifle. He represented the Carter budget. The second was a four-eyed wimp who looked like Woody Allen, carrying a tiny rifle. That was [Stockman's] budget. Finally there was "GI Joe himself, 190 pounds of fighting man, all decked out in helmet and flak jacket and pointing an M-60 machine gun. . . . This imposing warrior represented, yes, the Department of Defense budget plan."

Stockman professed disbelief that "a Harvard-educated cabinet officer" could have brought this intellectually "disreputable and demeaning" argument before the president. "Did he think the White House was on Sesame Street?" But Weinberger had the president's ear and Reagan approved the higher level of military spending. In 1986, annual Defense Department outlays peaked at just over $300 billion. Even this sum did not include large military expenditures contained in the budgets of the CIA, Department of Energy, and National Security Agency.

Economic Seesaw

An economic recession, the worst since the 1930s, began late in 1981 and lasted almost two years. Unemployment rose to over 10%, the highest rate since the Second World War, while business failures, farm foreclosures, and homelessness increased dramatically. By November 1982, over 11.5 million Americans had lost jobs and as many as 10 million others were forced into lower paying work. In the election that month, the Republicans lost 26 seats in the House but retained control of the Senate.

The president, whose standing in opinion polls bottomed out at 35% in January 1983, urged Congress and the American people to "stay the course." He blamed the recession and growing budget deficit on problems inherited from Carter and on the tight money policies (which he privately endorsed) pushed by Federal Reserve chairman Paul Volcker.

As Reagan predicted, the economy turned around in 1983. The inflation rate declined from about 14% in 1980 to under 2% in

1983. Interest rates gradually declined from 21% to a still histori-cally high 11%. Declining prices for imported oil also stimulated the economy. Between 1983 and 1989, 18 million new jobs were created. The average price of stocks nearly tripled in value.

The Reagan administration insisted that this recovery resulted from tax cuts and private, not public, spending. This is not clear. Between 1982 and 1989, the combined effects of the defense buildup and the financing of the growing budget deficit pumped several hundred billion dollars annually into the economy. These expen-ditures tended to have a regional impact, for example, creating a boom in the high technology and aerospace industry in New En-gland, the Southwest, and West Coast.

Relaxed banking rules (discussed in Chapter 4) prompted savings and loan institutions to provide easy, federally insured credit to commercial builders and land speculators. Business got an addi-tional boost from deregulation. In the late 1970s, the Carter ad-ministration began eliminating federal regulations that interfered with competition. Prices in the airline, telephone, and trucking in-dustry, kept at artificially high levels, declined. The Reagan admin-istration saw virtually all regulation, including those which man-dated worker and consumer safety, or clean air and water, as anti-competitive. Federal agencies abolished requirements for such things as stronger car bumpers and environmental restraints on offshore oil drilling.

Agencies including the Occupational Health and Safety Admin-istration (OSHA), Environmental Protection Agency (EPA), Se-curities Exchange Commission, and bank regulatory commissions suffered a double blow. Reagan appointed agency heads, such as Anne Gorsuch Burford of EPA, and James Watt of the Depart-ment of the Interior, hostile to the concept of regulation. Budgets were slashed, resulting in staff shortages that made it difficult to enforce existing rules.

It can be argued that massive federal expenditures for defense, deficit financing, easier credit and relaxed regulation, rather than market forces, pulled the nation out of recession and funded the recovery that lasted through 1990. When Reagan left office, a large majority of Americans agreed that the final six years of his term marked a period of broad prosperity.

The Great Communicator

Reagan, as journalist Lou Cannon noted, was not believable because he was a "Great Communicator." He was a "Great Communicator because he was believable." The president sounded persuasive mouthing inspirational homilies because he believed in them. He had no doubt about the simple "truth" embodied in his vision of a pre-urban, homogeneous nation where hard work and private charity were all that anyone needed in an unthreatening world. Millions of Americans, consciously or unconsciously, looked to Reagan to restore the security of that "lost world."

Reagan achieved his most important legislative successes during his first two years in office. (The one major exception was the tax reform of 1986, discussed below.) Chief of Staff James Baker shepherded the tax and spending cuts as well as defense increases through Congress. Assistant Chief of Staff Michael Deaver masterfully promoted Reagan's image through the media. Counselor Edwin Meese served as the president's conservative lightning rod. Still, minus the chief executive's unique relationship with the public, no amount of "packaging" would have succeeded.

Reagan perfected what some historians have called the "ceremonial presidency." With his ruddy good looks, the richness and tremor in his voice, and a twinkle in his eye, he fulfilled an ideal of what a president should be. He told corny jokes and inspirational stories so well that few listeners complained when he repeated them. Sophisticated critics snickered at his cliches and factual errors, dismissing him as a creature of the teleprompter. Some observers noted that the constant stream of jokes and anecdotes often served to deflect serious questions or any introspection. But these criticisms ignored the magnetism of Reagan's bond with the American public.

For one thing, the president's style was especially effective on TV. Television had become the source of news for most Americans. The number of people who read a daily newspaper declined dramatically during the 1980s. Overall, the readership decreased from 73% to 50%. For those aged 18–29, readership declined from 60% to 29%. Television news coverage itself increasingly resembled entertainment. CBS's "60 Minutes" paved the way for NBC's

"Real People." Just a small step led the media to the pseudo-news presented by entertainers like Geraldo Rivera. Television also promoted a hybrid of fact and fiction called "docudramas." These re-enactments of historical events usually emphasized the personal quirks of influential people, often with little basis in fact.

Short, snappy commercials and constant channel flipping ("grazing") facilitated by remote control devices shortened the attention span of viewers. Background images, rather than words affected the audience most viscerally. Reagan's emphasis on ephemeral, soothing words and images of renewal were perfect for television.

The White House staff formulated presidential speeches to appeal to the emotions of television viewers, not the intellect of concerned citizens. Pollster Richard Wirthlin tested themes by measuring the "speech pulse" of selected audiences. Utilizing a technique developed for assessing television scripts, the test group listened to a Reagan stand-in read a draft speech while they fingered computerized dials. Later, Wirthlin studied a printout listing the text on one side and a word-by-word audience response on the other. He identified "power phrases" that elicited the most positive responses. These were included in later drafts while less evocative words were omitted.

During Reagan's first term, this kind of media management worked nearly flawlessly. Assistant Chief of Staff Michael Deaver (who once declared: "I am Ronald Reagan. . . . Every morning after I get up I make believe I am him and ask what he should do and where he should go") and Communications Director David Gergen rewrote the rules of presidential image making. While some presidents, such as Richard Nixon, tried to manipulate the press by intimidating it, Reagan's staff embraced journalists with trivia as a way of controlling them.

For example, each morning White House staff set the "line of the day," which all high officials were expected to stress in their press contacts. Deaver made certain that the print and electronic media had frequent opportunities to photograph Reagan doing something. He arranged nearly every presidential action as a possible spot on the evening news or a front-page newspaper picture. Presidential appearances, one journalist noted, were "conceived . . . in terms of camera angle." Although he was the most photographed of presidents (on average, the White House released four to six thousand pictures of Reagan per month), photo opportunities merely created the illusion of openness and accessibility to reporters. During his first year in office, he held six press conferences, a record low for modern presidents. Reporters were reduced to shouting questions in his direction while camera crews recorded him greeting visitors or boarding a helicopter.

In 1984 correspondent Leslie Stahl ran a feature on CBS news that contrasted Reagan's attendance at the Handicapped Olympics with the fact that he pushed Congress into cutting federal support for the handicapped. A short time after the story aired, a White House staffer thanked Stahl for the "great piece," calling it a "five-minute commercial" for the president. Stahl objected. "Didn't you hear what I said?" Richard Darmon replied, "Nobody heard what you said. They just saw the five minutes of beautiful pictures of Ronald Reagan. They saw the balloons, they saw the flags, they saw the red, white and blue. Haven't you people figured out yet that the picture always overrides what you say?"

Each morning Chief of Staff James Baker (later, Donald Regan) informed Reagan about that day's "line" and handed him a set of index cards. These contained the day's schedule, jokes to tell visitors, and the text of both casual and formal statements. The cards even indicated where he should stand at various ceremonies in order to assure the best photo opportunities. Leaving nothing to chance, the president's aides even scripted the phrase "God Bless you," that Reagan used to end most speeches. The ever-present cue cards, Donald Regan later commented, were "sort of like Linus's blue blanket."

Reagan's evocation of simple patriotic themes generated among Americans a sense of community and a renewed identification with government. The president's self-confidence made him appear an effective leader, irrespective of where he led. Unlike Carter, Reagan usually got Congress to act on his terms. His grins, jokes, and anecdotes wore down the most hardbitten politicians. Even Tip O'Neill, the Democratic Speaker of the House who opposed nearly all Reagan's policies, admitted that after 6 P.M., he liked sitting down to swap Irish stories with the president. If charm failed, Reagan appealed directly to the American people via television.

Several times in 1981 his request that citizens call and write their representatives turned around close votes.

Reagan had an instinctive ability to reassure and soothe the feelings of grieving Americans in the aftermath of tragedy. For example, following the disastrous explosion of the space shuttle *Challenger* in January 1986, the president's moving eulogy, written by Peggy Noonan, stressed the theme of renewal. The astronauts had "slipped the surly bonds of earth to touch the face of God." A grateful nation would reach out for new goals, and even greater achievements in order to commemorate "our seven Challenger heros."

In a similar vein, Reagan personalized the sacrifice of veterans during his 1984 visit to the Normandy battlefield. He embraced aging survivors of the D-Day invasion and linked a younger generation to the heroism of the old. The president's speechwriter drew heavily from a letter sent by the daughter of a soldier in which she recalled her father's hope of someday returning to the battlefield. But he had died before making the visit and his daughter, Lisa Zanatta Henn, asked if she could attend the anniversary celebration on his behalf.

Quoting the letter, with Ms. Henn as his guest, Reagan told an audience on the Normandy bluffs how Private Peter Zanatta, an ordinary American, the child of immigrants, had fought bravely to liberate Europe. Despite the death of his comrades, Zanatta told his daughter he had merely "did what you had to do and you kept on going." Reagan recited Henn's promise to her father: "I'll never forget what you went through, Dad, nor will I let anyone else forget. And Dad, I'll always be proud." Framed by the sky, sea, and rows of white crosses on countless graves, Reagan saluted the sacrifice of those who helped crush Hitler. "We will always remember. We will always be proud. We will always be prepared, so we may always be free." Millions of Americans gulped as he brushed a tear from his eye.

Between 1960 and 1980, five presidential administrations had ended in failure. Reagan and his closest first-term advisers—James A. Baker, Michael Deaver, and Edwin Meese—sensed the public's strong desire to see a president succeed and understood that the media could play a critical role in assuring success. This triumvir-

President and Mrs. Reagan at a cemetery on the Normandy battle-field. *Courtesy U.S. National Archives.*

ate, one administration official commented, believed "reality happened once a day, on the evening news. They never read anything. They lived off the tube."

Ben Bradlee, editor of the *Washington Post,* believed his paper, like many others, was "kinder to President Reagan than any president that I can remember." Some liberal journalists felt they had to give the benefit of the doubt to a popular conservative. Michael Deaver agreed that for most of his two terms, "Ronald Reagan enjoyed the most generous treatment by the press of any president in the postwar era."

Reagan had the actor's knack of convincing an audience to suspend disbelief by becoming true believers in his own claim that saying something made it so. At the same time, he often thought that merely proclaiming a policy was the same as seeing it well and faithfully executed. Even when enterprising journalists exposed statistical mis-statements or faulty facts, the public forgave Reagan's errors as a sign he was a kindly man who had trouble with complex statistics.

The president made a point of inviting people he called "ordinary American heroes" as his guests on public occasions. These citizens had performed impulsive acts of courage, like saving accident victims, or were exemplars of private charity. In celebrating these individual achievements, Reagan connected government—and himself—to the public and also sent a message that government need not be counted upon to solve problems.

Reagan's consistently cheery demeanor—his "Mr. Magoo style," as biographer Garry Wills called it—and his staff's skills usually salvaged mis-steps before they became major embarrassments. After his administration announced plans to reduce federal aid to education, pollsters detected strong voter opposition. Michael Deaver then arranged for Reagan to deliver a series of speeches on "excellence in education" and arranged for a Rose Garden ceremony where the president honored a "teacher of the year." Peggy Noonan composed his remarks by paraphrasing lines spoken by Sir Thomas More in the play *A Man for All Seasons*. When a bright young man asks More who will know it if he proves a good teacher, More responds: "You, your students, God. Not a bad audience that." The White House and NASA also promoted a "teacher in space program" as a sign of Reagan's support for education. Opinion surveys found a two-to-one swing in favor of the president's stand on education, despite the fact that none of the funding cuts were restored.

At one point Reagan expressed his belief that corporations should not be taxed. A strong public backlash worried Deaver who promptly rushed the president to a working-class bar in Boston where he hoisted a few beers with the regulars. Cameras were positioned so the scene resembled the hit show "Cheers." The issue soon faded from discussion.

Ronald Reagan supplied the vision, voice, and good looks while an inner coterie of advisers managed the nation's affairs. Even the president's closest allies admitted that he remained detached from most details of governing. His skill lay in "salesmanship," what George Bush called the "vision thing," not strategy or tactics. Reagan was neither a phoney nor a dunce, but someone who lived in a world composed more of symbols and myths than facts and programs. Through him, many Americans discovered a link to a simpler past. He allowed people to feel that anything was possible, as in a daydream.

Reagan limited his attention to a handful of issues, such as cutting taxes, promoting the Strategic Defense Initiative (SDI), and speaking out against abortion. As speechwriter Peggy Noonan observed, "taxes and SDI and abortion were issues that captured his imagination. He could see how taxes hurt . . . he could see how SDI, with a perfectly directed laser beam, could shoot down a missile . . . he could see the fetus kicking away from the needle." Once he imagined these things, he could not abandon them.

Reagan reveled in the ceremonial functions of office. His staff discovered how much he loved the trappings of the presidency, such as the helicopters at his command, the parades, and reviewing troops. Only the presentation of the National Thanksgiving Turkey—a bird slated for the oven—made him uncomfortable. "Every moment of every public appearance," Chief of Staff Donald Regan recalled, "was scheduled, every word was scripted, every place where Reagan was expected to stand was chalked with toe marks. . . . He had been learning his lines, composing his facial expression, hitting his toe marks for half a century." At one point, the president told his press spokesman, Larry Speakes, that he was happiest when "each morning I get a piece of paper that tells me what I do all day long." He felt his job was "something like shooting a script" in which characters appeared, departed, and the plot advanced.

Although some people speculate that a man well into his seventies might falter under the burdens of office, the presidency did not tax Reagan mentally or physically. He worked a nine-to-five shift that included an afternoon nap. He took frequent three-day weekends at Camp David and punctuated the season with many vacations. As noted, these included 345 days spent on his California ranch. To make it appear that he worked harder, the White House staff released a false daily schedule that showed him working long hours. His nap was listed as "personal staff time."

Kenneth Duberstein, who served as Reagan's last chief of staff in 1988–89, noted that an actor-politician like his boss required a "very strong stage manager-producer-director." His presidency needed "very good technical men and sound men at all times." When the talent was not there, everything "falls apart because the actor-president isn't prepared."

So poised in scripted settings, Reagan seemed uninformed about many of his programs. Infrequent and impromptu news conferences, where his partial deafness and unexpected questions often confused him, were painful to watch—and kept to a minimum. One time, when a reporter asked him to describe administration arms control policies, he drew a blank. Nancy Reagan whispered in her husband's ear: "Tell them we're doing all we can." He dutifully repeated the phrase.

Occasionally, Reagan said nothing at all but was still quoted in the press. For example, White House spokesman Larry Speakes considered it important for the media to print a statesmanlike phrase from the president on important topics of the day. So when Reagan failed to say something suitable, Speakes simply supplied the words himself.

Staff members admitted that Reagan appeared lethargic, had difficult in learning the names of subordinates or foreign officials, and tended to nod off during meetings. One memorable photograph caught him dozing during a talk by visiting Pope John Paul II. Yet, Reagan's ability to charm potential critics with self-mockery staved off ridicule. In response to critics who complained about his on-the-job napping, he joked that his chair in the Cabinet room might someday bear the label "Ronald Reagan slept here."

Much of the criticism leveled against Reagan by Democrats, liberals, and minorities charged him with being "unfair" or "insensitive" to those in need. The President dismissed this as pleading by "special interests." He had broken up their "Washington buddy system" and they could not forgive him. This was, of course, partly true.

But a large measure of Reagan's appeal was based on his easy charm, not his talent or accomplishment. Dr. Oliver Sachs, a neurophysiologist and author of the bestselling case study *The Man Who Mistook His Wife for a Hat* (1985) observed the critical reaction to Reagan's speeches among patients in his hospital's aphasia ward.

There he was, the old Charmer, the Actor, with his practiced rhetoric, his histrionisms, his emotional appeal—and all the patients
were convulsed with laughter . . . The president was, as always,
moving—but he was moving them, apparently mainly to laughter.
What could they be thinking? Were they failing to understand him?
Or did they, perhaps, understand him all too well?

Aphasiacs, Sachs explains, experience an elevated understanding
of the "tone color" of language, the quality of speech that com-
municates an inner meaning rather than the mere assemblage of
words. One cannot lie to an aphasiac because he cannot compre-
hend your words, and so is not deceived by them. But victims of
aphasia grasp with "infallible precision . . . the *expression* that goes
with the words." An aphasiac perceives the verisimilitude of a
speaker's voice and cannot suspend disbelief. Reagan's "grimaces,
the histrionisms, the false gestures, and above all, the false tones
and cadences of the voice . . . rang false for these immensely sensitive patients."

For Sachs, the reaction of these brain-damaged adults represented the "paradox" of Reagan's appeal. Normal audiences, "aided
doubtless by our wish to be fooled, were indeed well and truly
fooled." The president's cunning and "deceptive" use of words
and tones assured that "only the brain-damaged remained intact,
undeceived."

Re-election and the Second Administration

The improving economy of 1983–84 revived Ronald Reagan's popularity. The average wage earner took home a few additional after-
tax dollars, inflation practically disappeared, and abstractions such
as the growing budget deficit were someone else's problem or, as
Reagan now argued, not really a problem at all. The president scored
a whopping success in invading tiny Grenada in 1983 (see Chapter
5) and shared the glory of the large number of gold medals won
by American athletes in the 1984 summer Olympics in Los Angeles.

The Democratic Party seemed rudderless, attempting to mobilize an electorate out of tune with its New Deal legacy. Civil rights activist Jesse Jackson urged the Party to reach out to the poor and disenfranchised of all races. He believed that by increasing the voter pool (rather than winning more votes among the 50% of the electorate who went to the polls) a Democrat could win the White House. Jackson proclaimed himself representative of a racially diverse "Rainbow Coalition" but the bulk of his following came from the African-American community. His association with Black Muslims and record of anti-Semitic remarks (such as calling New York "Hymie-Town") alarmed many whites, Jews, and other European ethnics who were key elements of the Democratic coalition.

Another "outsider," Senator Gary Hart of Colorado, also urged Democrats to reach beyond their New Deal past. Young, handsome, articulate, and telegenic, Hart spoke about "New Ideas" (though revealed few) and said meeting the future mattered more than shopworn ideology. In pursuit of the nomination, he reached out to young, urban, socially liberal, economically conservative voters, dubbed "yuppies."

Former Vice President Walter Mondale, in comparison, sought support from traditional Democratic strongholds, such as organized labor, ethnic organizations, women's groups, teachers, environmentalists, and other progressive elements in the Democratic Party. Critics derided Mondale's celebration of the glory days of the Democrats as well as his quest for endorsements, as pandering to "special interests." Nevertheless, Mondale accumulated enough support to win the nomination. Mondale hoped to energize his candidacy by making a visible display of considering running mates drawn from a broad list of men, women, northerners, southerners, pro-labor Democrats, and ethnic minorities. Yet critics labeled his talent hunt as simply new evidence that he was beholden to "special interests."

He finally selected New York Congresswoman Geraldine Ferarro to share the ticket. As the first woman nominated for vice president by a major party, Ferarro excited millions of Americans. Smart and articulate, she easily held her own in debate with Vice President George Bush. Questions raised about her husband's financial dealings, however, obscured her critique of the Reagan presidency. Some voters worried that having served only three terms in Congress, Ferarro was "untested." In the end, her presence on the ticket failed to help.

Mondale tried to run a campaign of issues, alerting the public to runaway spending, a spiraling arms race, environmental disasters, and the unfairness of Reagan's economic policies. His most telling campaign line was "He'll raise taxes, so will I. He won't tell you, I just did." For a few days, commentators praised his political courage. Within a week he was labeled a political suicide. Republicans like UN ambassador Jeane Kirkpatrick dubbed "bad news Fritz Mondale" a wimp and part of the "blame America first crowd."

Nor could Mondale compete with Reagan's personality appeal. The Democratic nominee looked gray on TV and sounded like a whiner. Mondale's droopy eyes (which the lighting that Reagan's media advisers selected for the televised debate exaggerated) and droning voice exuded as much pessimism as Reagan generated optimism. His association with the ill-fated Carter doomed him. Even though the incumbent performed badly in a first debate, by the second round Reagan returned in grand form. He heaped one-line jokes on the challenger, even turning aside concerns about his age with the remark: "I am not going to exploit, for political purpose, my opponent's youth and inexperience." Like Carter, Mondale learned belatedly how effective the Reagan treatment could be.

In his speeches and commercials, the president promoted themes of redemption, patriotism, and family. "We see an America," he declared, "where everyday is independence day, the Fourth of July." One memorable television ad included a montage of Reagan at the Normandy battlefield, wiping a tear from his eye. Embracing the now elderly veterans, the president remarked "the best damned kids in the world." Another TV spot showed Reagan at the border between North and South Korea, grimly staring into communist territory. A third pictured him embracing Olympic champions, while a voice proclaimed "America Is Coming Back!" In one elaborate production, a cowboy stood in for the president, looking much like the fabled "Marlboro Man" of earlier cigarette commercials. As he wiped dust off his clothes he remarked "we rolled up our sleeves and showed that [in] working together there is nothing we Americans can't do." As usual, the message evoked the idea of tradition and community.

Mondale reflected, with some bitterness, that while "he tried to discuss issues, Reagan patted dogs." Nevertheless, the incumbent's "feel good" campaign yielded a personal triumph. Reagan won majorities in 49 states. At the same time Democratic candidates for state and federal office ran far ahead of Mondale. The Democrats retained their majority in the House and pecked av y at the slim Republican majority in the Senate. Reagan's coat tails proved surprisingly short, despite his victory.

Second-Term Complications

Despite Reagan's re-election triumph, internal staff changes, whiffs of scandal, and a foreign policy debacle began to diminish Reagan's lustre. Trouble began after the talented White House Chief of Staff, James Baker, decided to leave his job. He and Treasury Secretary Donald Regan decided between themselves to switch jobs. They made the deal first and presented it for the president's approval later.

The new Chief of Staff, Donald Regan, discovered that the president seldom discussed policy matters. Nor were Regan's gut instincts helpful. He lacked James Baker's political finesse with Congress and got along badly with First Lady Nancy Reagan. This became the source of much trouble.

Early in the second administration, Assistant Chief of Staff Michael Deaver and Presidential Counselor Edwin Meese also left the White House. Deaver, anxious to cash in on his access to powerful officials, opened a public relations firm and fell afoul of influence-peddling laws. Eventually, he was convicted of lying to Congress about his lobbying activities. Another close associate of the president, Lyn Nofziger, also went into the lobbying business after leaving his White House job. Convicted of violating the Ethics in Government Act, Nofziger's sentence was later overturned on appeal.

Edwin Meese seemed constantly in trouble after the president nominated him to became Attorney General. Reports alleged that he filed false tax returns, retained stock in companies doing business with the Justice Department, and received illegal payoffs from parties seeking government favors. The most damaging allegations involved Meese's ties to his close friend and financial adviser, E. Robert Wallach. As discussed in Chapter 4, Wallach worked as a consultant for a corrupt defense contracting firm called Wedtech corporation. Lengthy investigations by the Senate and by a special prosecutor concluded that Meese exercised terrible judgment, had technically violated the law, but that "insufficient evidence" existed to warrant his indictment. With the president riding high in opinion polls and still wanting Meese to head the Justice Department, the Senate confirmed him. These and other problems dogging administration officials were dubbed the "sleaze factor."

Early in 1985, a minor faux pas became an international embarrassment. Aware that Reagan planned to attend a European economic conference, West German Chancellor Helmut Kohl invited him to speak in Germany on the theme of reconciliation. As one of his final assignments before leaving the White House, Michael Deaver approved a presidential address at the military cemetery in Bitburg. Shortly after the announcement, it became known that forty-seven Nazi Waffen SS troops—Hitler's chosen elite—were buried along with ordinary soldiers. Veterans of all the Allied powers, Jewish groups, and over half the members of the U.S. Senate urged Reagan to speak somewhere else.

To everyone's amazement, the president balked. Perhaps this reflected his actor's maxim of never cancelling an appearance once the billing became public. In any case, Reagan downplayed the guilt of the stormtroopers (he later claimed that he did "research" which showed that many in the SS had opposed Hitler!), declared that few people remembered the war anyway, and suggested that all those killed in the war were equal victims of Nazism. "Somehow," a battered White House aide remarked, "we have accomplished the impossible. We have even got the American Legion to criticize Ronald Reagan."

Once the president had dug in his heels, Nancy Reagan tried to control the damage. She arranged for her husband to shorten the Bitburg visit and follow it with a speech at the Bergen-Belsen concentration camp, where many felt Hitler's true victims had perished. The First Lady consulted her astrologer, Joan Quigley, about the precise timing of the two visits, changing the schedule numerous times as Quigley reinterpreted the data.¹ When Michael Deaver complained about rescheduling the president as he traveled between the two sites, Nancy Reagan declared, "I'm talking about my husband's life!" Trying to please both Mrs. Reagan and "Madame Zorba," as Deaver called Quigley, sometimes made the assistant chief of staff's job a "nightmare."

By the summer of 1986, Reagan recovered his poise. The stock market surged to record levels. Congress passed a major tax reform, the economic centerpiece of his second term. The new tax law, a modification of a "flat" income tax rate proposed by Democrats Bill Bradley and Richard Gephardt, was touted as a means of restoring simplicity and equality to the tax code. It closed many loopholes and reduced multiple tax brackets to just three: 15, 28, and 33%. The law eliminated taxes for the poorest Americans, but a quirk in the code allowed the wealthiest Americans to pay a tax rate slightly below the upper middle class. Ultimately, most people paid about the same as they had before the law changed. Yet, Reagan claimed, and many accepted his assertion, that the law reduced federal taxes.

On July 4, 1986, the president hosted a birthday party for the refurbished Statue of Liberty. The patriotic extravaganza, which included the biggest fireworks display ever assembled, showed off Ronald Reagan at his best. As Leslie Stahl, White House reporter for CBS, commented, "Like his leading lady, the Statute of Liberty, the president, after six years in office, has himself become a symbol of pride in America." *Time* called the event proof of Reagan's "Yankee Doodle Magic."

Yet, for all Reagan's personal magnetism, he failed to engineer a

¹Mrs. Reagan, like her husband, was superstitious and had frequently consulted astrologers about auspicious times for travel, making decisions, and holding ceremonies. After the president's brush with death in 1981, family friend Merv Griffin recommended she rely upon Joan Quigley, an astrologer in San Francisco. By 1985 Nancy Reagan believed that Quigley's advice about what days and hours were auspicious for her husband to travel had prevented him from falling victim to a second assassin. Donald Regan revealed this relationship, and the havoc it played in White House schedules, in his 1988 memoir *For the Record*. Joan Quigley describes her relationship with the Reagans in considerable detail in her 1990 memoir *What Does Joan Say?*

major realignment in American politics below the presidential level. Despite his high approval ratings, the Democrats actually regained control of the Senate and picked up additional House seats in the November 1986 election. Again in control of both houses of Congress, and with Reagan a lame duck, the Democrats blocked administration proposals to further cut social programs, expand defense spending, or intervene more directly in Central American conflicts.

Still unclear at the time of the election, Reagan had authorized a series of weapons-for-hostage deals with Iran, a country classified as a terrorist state. In tune with the president's theatricality, some of his staff had hoped to arrange the release of Americans held in Beirut in time for their surprise appearance at the Statue of Liberty unveiling on July 4, 1986. Members of the National Security Council convinced the president to pursue a convoluted secret scheme to ransom hostages in Lebanon and use arms sale profits to finance anti-communist guerrillas in Nicaragua. The Iran-Contra scandal, which became public at the end of 1986 and is discussed in the concluding chapters, nearly toppled the Reagan administration.

As Congress, the courts, and public opinion sorted out the Iran-Contra scandal, a collapse in stock prices during October 1987 rattled the "don't worry, be happy" economic mood prevailing since 1983. In August 1987, the Dow Jones average hit a record high of 2,700 points and then began to weaken. In mid-October it fell 600 points in a few days, losing almost a fourth of its value and reviving fears of the 1929 stock market crisis that ushered in the Great Depression. Computer-driven stock trading programs and inadequate regulation made the problem worse. Wall Street recovered most of its losses within a year, but the mini-crash suggested that the Reagan boom rested on a shaky foundation.

Both the president's critics and supporters suspected that the Iran-Contra scandal and stock crash might become Reagan's epitaph. But his good luck and ability to adjust to circumstances once again surprised Americans. During 1988 relations between the United States and the Soviet Union, which had deteriorated since 1981, improved dramatically, creating the possibility for an end to the Cold War. Internal economic and political problems almost certainly accounted for the changes in Soviet policies. But the fact that superpower relations improved during "Reagan's watch" naturally allowed him to take much of the credit.

The public responded enthusiastically to the thaw in the Cold War, suppressing economic anxieties and recrimination about Reagan's arms deals with Iran. Following a series of dramatic meetings with Soviet leader Mikhail Gorbachev, the president's stature soared. In addition, Reagan could point to promises he fulfilled. He had pledged to cut income taxes, boost military spending, and make Americans "feel good." As far as most people were concerned, he accomplished all three goals. When he retired in January 1989, over 70% of Americans gave him a favorable rating, a higher total than any president since Franklin Roosevelt, who died in office.

Ronald Reagan enjoyed telling an anecdote that he believed refuted the "gloom and doom" naysayers who doubted he would achieve his goals. He described two boys, a pessimist and an optimist, who received Christmas gifts. The pessimist got a roomful of toys, but still felt miserable because he was sure there had to be a catch. The optimist got a roomful of horse manure but seemed delighted. He dug around for hours, explaining "that with all that manure, there just had to be a pony in there somewhere!"

The story epitomized the president's charm and his own optimism as well as his failure to recognize that both boys lived in something of a fantasy world. Reagan's greatest achievement was restoring a sense of national pride and optimism among many Americans as well as presiding over a modest economic expansion. He challenged the liberal consensus prevailing since the 1930s and brought conservative economic and social thought into the political mainstream. But in domestic as well as foreign policy, as we will see, Reagan left a complicated, often contradictory, legacy.

3

Rhetoric, Reality, and Results: The Reagan Years at Home

R ONALD REAGAN had an impact on American government and society that was both less than he claimed and greater than his critics admitted. The president took credit for what he called the longest post-1945 period of economic growth, a reduction in the size, cost, and scope of government, a rebirth of national spirit, and the restoration of "traditional" values in such varied spheres as judicial decision making and private moral behavior. Administration policies affected all this and more, although not always in ways Reagan understood.

Late in 1987, about the time the collapse in stock prices rocked the Reagan Recovery, director Oliver Stone released the film *Wall Street,* a cautionary tale about the rise and fall of a tycoon named Gordon Gekko. Gekko specialized in buying up shares in undervalued companies through "leveraged buyouts," a fancy term for borrowed money. To finance the deals, he sold off, or "stripped," assets of the acquired corporation, reaping large personal profits. Often, however, little remained of the original company. In a climactic scene, a group of stockholders opposed to Gekko's acquisition of an airline berates him for his greed and fixation with profits. With disdain, Gekko retorts that "greed is good, greed is healthy" because it promotes growth and success in the free market. In the end, however, Gekko is exposed as a crook who se-

The Great Communicator leads the Pledge of Allegiance. *Courtesy U.S. National Archives.*

cretly broke the law to build his fortune. This parable of deceit was, in fact, a case of art imitating life.

In May 1986 financier Ivan F. Boesky—the Gekko prototype—addressed, for the second time that year, graduating business students at the University of California at Berkeley. At forty-eight years of age, Boesky was already a legend among aspiring MBAs. The child of immigrant parents, he earned over $100 million in 1985 buying underpriced shares of stock in companies about to be acquired in lucrative mergers. Boesky summarized his recent book, *Merger Mania*, by saying that his success reflected the tried and true virtues of hard work, common sense, and luck. "There are no easy ways to make money in the securities market," he observed. Boesky assured the students that "greed is healthy." Earning and flaunting great wealth was the mother's milk of capitalism, growth, and prosperity. The audience sat rapt as he recited the canon of the free market. He admonished them that as they "accumulated wealth and power," they ought to remain "God-fearing and responsible to the system that has given you this opportunity." They should "give back to the system with humility, and don't take yourself too seriously."

In November 1986 the Securities Exchange Commission and New York prosecutors announced that Ivan Boesky had pled guilty to illegally buying "inside" information from corporate officials which he used to manipulate stock prices, acquire companies, and earn a fortune. As part of the plea bargain, Boesky paid a civil fine of $100 million (half of which was tax deductible), pled guilty to a criminal charge which carried up to five years in prison, and promised to cooperate in the prosecution of corrupt business associates. In several important ways, Boesky's rise and fall mirrored the ambiguities of the Reagan era.

Economic Imbalances

Economic growth during the Reagan Recovery proved highly selective. In general, prosperity and wealth flowed to the East and West coasts, partly because of defense spending. The Northeast and California thrived even as farm and energy-producing regions stagnated. After having been given up for dead in the 1970s, Boston and Manhattan blossomed during the 1980s. Real estate values skyrocketed for both residential and commercial property.

In contrast, the so-called rust belt of the upper Midwest experienced a loss of high-paying industrial jobs. The steel industry, for example, lost over $12 billion during the 1980s. Employment fell by 58%. Even as Reagan spoke of "morning in America," the sun began to set on traditional industries such as steel, rubber, machine tools, and automobile manufacturing. Farmers also faced hard times. Following a boom in the 1970s, land value declined as did the prices farmers received for their products. By mid-decade, farm income declined to a point below where it had been in 1970. The country avoided a national recession between 1983 and 1989, but rolling, regional recessions were common phenomena.

In his first economic message as president, Reagan blamed the Democrats for mortgaging the future to finance current consumption. By the mid-1980s, Democratic politicians and many economists charged that Reagan had placed the federal government on the equivalent of a credit-card buying binge. Instead of "tax and spend liberals," "borrow and spend conservatives," dominated government.

Both the government and private industry thrived on unprecedented levels of indebtedness. During Reagan's two terms the cumulative national debt tripled, from about $900 billion to almost $2.7 trillion. Interest payments alone cost taxpayers $200 billion per year. Government borrowing absorbed three-fourths of the annual net savings of families and businesses. In light of this, some cynics labeled Reagan's talk of balanced budgets a "classic case of a drunk preaching temperance."

The domestic borrowing pool had to be supplemented by large infusions of foreign capital, especially from Japan and Germany. By the late-1980s, foreign investors held as much as 20% of the national debt. In less than a decade, the United States went from being the world's biggest creditor to the world's biggest debtor. Instead of interest payments on the debt flowing into private American coffers, a growing portion of the payments flowed out of the country.

The nation's foreign trade deficit also grew dramatically during the 1980s. Near the start of the decade, the value of foreign manufactured imports surpassed by about $26 billion the value of American manufactured products sold abroad. By the end of the decade, the United States ran a deficit of more than $150 billion per year. Every week, on average during the 1980s, American consumers spent about $2 billion more abroad than foreigners spent on American products. The cumulative trade imbalance for the decade approached $1 trillion.

Foreign investors used their dollar surpluses to buy American real estate, factories, and stock shares. Some economists considered this a healthy vote of confidence. Foreign investments provided jobs for Americans. But business profits—and decision-making power—flowed abroad. Economic security depended increasingly on Japanese, British, German, Dutch, and Saudi willingness to buy the public and private debt of the United States.

The New Federalism

As a presidential candidate, Ronald Reagan pledged to shrink the scope of the federal government by returning greater authority and responsibility to the states. In practice, the Reagan administration shifted costs, not power, to local government. Under the so-called "new federalism," Washington burdened state, county, and city governments with many new, expensive to administer regulations, such as monitoring pollution, removing asbestos from schools, and supervising nursing homes—but provided less federal money than before.

During the 1980s, federal allocations to states fell by almost 13%, from $109 to $94 billion calculated in constant 1982 dollars. As Carroll A. Campbell, Jr., the Republican governor of South Carolina, complained: "instead of giving power to the states and giving us the flexibility of addressing problems," the states had new federal mandates imposed upon them. Even though state officials often agreed with the purpose of the new mandates (such as controlling pollution), they considered the Reagan administration's denial of funds a "cruel deception."

Other forms of cost cutting affected states negatively. For example, federal agencies postponed repairs of highways, bridges, and other parts of the transportation system to save money. These savings were really costs passed down to those who followed. Far from sharing in the "Reagan Recovery," by 1989 half the fifty states listed themselves as suffering from "fiscal distress." To pay for vital services, many states raised taxes. This negated a large part of the federal income tax reduction.

The Culture of Greed

Supply-siders certainly achieved their goal of reversing New Deal style income redistribution programs. Not only did resources cease to flow from wealthier to less well off Americans, but a substantial portion of national wealth was redistributed to Germany and Japan. Reagan-era policies practically doubled the share of national income going to the wealthiest 1% of Americans, from 8.1 to about 15%. In 1980, 4,400 individuals filed income tax returns reporting an adjusted gross income of over $1 million. By 1987, over 35,000 taxpayers filed such returns. The net worth of the 400 richest Americans nearly tripled. In 1980 a typical corporate chief executive officer (CEO) made about 40 times the income of an average factory worker, nine years later the CEO made 93 times as much. Lawyers handling business mergers also gained great wealth. Over 1,300 partners of major law firms averaged higher pay than the 800 top executives in industry.

Not since the Gilded Age of the late nineteenth century or the Roaring Twenties had the acquisition and flaunting of wealth been so publicly celebrated as during the 1980s. Income became the accepted measure of one's value to society. Professional athletes earned immense sums as teams scrambled to recruit basketball, football, and baseball players from colleges. Congressman Kemp, economist Laffer, and writers Jude Wanniski and George Gilder celebrated financiers and deal makers as secular saints, enriching society. In his bestselling book *Wealth and Poverty* (1981) and opinion pieces appearing in the *Wall Street Journal,* Gilder emerged as a theologian of capitalism. "Faith in man, faith in the future, faith in the rising returns of giving, faith in the mutual benefits of trade, faith in the providence of God are all essential to successful capitalism," he wrote. In the gospel according to Gilder, "Capitalism begins with giving . . . thus the contest of gifts leads to an expansion of human sympathies." Accumulating wealth represented the highest morality. Only the unsuccessful blamed the system for their problems. The poor of the 1980s, he claimed, "are refusing to work hard."

Gilder, Laffer, and Wanniski identified the true heros of the age as Wall Street operators such as Carl Icahn, T. Boone Pickens, Ivan Boesky, and Michael Milken and real estate speculator Donald Trump—men who earned billions of dollars buying and merging companies and in construction. They were celebrated as role models and builders of a better world.

A "merger mania," fueled by changes in the 1981 tax law and a

Donald Trump in front of his helicopter. *Courtesy AP/Wide World Photos.*

relaxed attitude toward enforcement of anti-trust statutes by the Reagan Justice Department, gripped Wall Street through 1987. Boesky and Milken exemplified the "risk arbitrageur," financiers who discovered ways to make fortunes by borrowing money to merge and acquire large enterprises. Many of the nation's biggest companies bought up competitors or were themselves swallowed up in leveraged buyouts, financed by huge loans bearing high interest rates. Corporate raiders argued that these deals rewarded stockholders and got rid of incompetent management, thus increasing competitiveness.

Because many multi-billion dollar deals were too risky for banks, insurance, or pension funds to finance, Milken and others pioneered the use of "junk bonds." Corporate raiders issued these I.O.U.s that paid very high rates of interest. Repayment of the heavy debt often compelled the purchaser to sell off or "strip" portions of the newly acquired business.

Many of the nation's largest corporations, including R. J. Reynolds, Nabisco, Walt Disney, Gulf, Federated Department Stores, and R.H. Macy were the objects of leveraged buyouts, some will-ingly and others under protest. Between 1984 and 1987, twenty-one mergers valued at over $1 billion each occurred. Many cor-porations sought to avoid hostile takeovers by boosting immediate profitability to stockholders by going heavily into debt through issuing bonds or paying special dividends. This increased indebt-edness made a buyout more expensive and less attractive to out-siders. It left the company less able to raise funds for investment in plants and new products.

Costly mergers did not necessarily or even usually produce a more competitive company. But immense profits were earned through arranging financing of the takeover, issuing junk bonds, or acting as a consultant to the deal. For example, in 1987 Michael Milken earned an estimated $550 million in fees. By age 40, he had become a billionaire.

Critics of these activities charged that money spent on acquisi-tions contributed nothing to the productive capacity of the econ-omy since it did not go into research or new product lines. The debt incurred by mergers became a long-term burden. Corporate profits went mainly to paying bondholders, not investing in new plants. In any period of recession, when profits dipped, it seemed likely that leveraged corporations would have difficulty paying in-terest on the costly junk bonds.

Following Boesky's conviction at the end of 1986, a series of probes revealed evidence of widespread insider trading among some of the most successful financiers. By the end of the decade Boesky, Milken, and many others pled guilty to a variety of illegal prac-tices. Drexel, Burnham, Lambert, Inc., Milken's trading firm and the giant of the junk bond industry, pled guilty to legal violations and went bankrupt. The junk bond market shrank dramatically by 1988, especially as heavily indebted companies began to default on payments and go into bankruptcy.

Yuppies

In mid-decade, a new social category emerged on the American scene. *Newsweek* magazine called 1984 "The Year of the Yuppie," an acronym for young, urban, upwardly mobile professionals. For a time, this group seemed as charmed as the Wall Street wizards. *Newsweek,* in particular, applauded the group's eagerness to "go for it" as a sign of the "yuppie virtues of imagination, daring and entrepreneurship." Yuppies existed "on a new plane of consciousness, a state of Transcendental Acquisition."

Demographers and advertisers first used the term. Journalists popularized it in 1983–84, partly to explain Senator Gary Hart's unexpected popularity among young Americans as he campaigned for the Democratic presidential nomination. Unlike radical protesters or hippies of the 1960s, these young adults were hardly social rebels. They plunged joyously into the American mainstream ready to consume.

Certified yuppies—people born between 1945 and 1959, earning over $40,000 as a professional or manager, and living in a city—totaled about 1.5 million. As candidate Hart learned, they were not a reliable constituency for Democratic liberals. Yuppies tended to be "pro-choice" on the abortion issue, enjoyed "recreational drugs," and supported Reagan's economic policies. They aspired to become investment bankers, not social workers. In 1985, for example, one-third of the entire senior class at Yale sought jobs as financial analysts at First Boston Corporation.

Yuppies enjoyed creature comforts, indulging themselves, when possible, with "leisure products" like Porsches and BMWs, expensive sneakers, state-of-the-art electronic equipment, and gourmet foods. They flocked to health spas, wore designer clothes made of natural fibers, jogged, and put a high value on "looking good."

Some commentators speculated that yuppies were merely reformed radicals from the 1960s. Superficially, some individuals conformed to this pattern. Former Black Panther Eldridge Cleaver returned from foreign exile, became a born-again Christian and clothing designer. Ex-Panther Bobby Seale, who once shouted "burn baby burn," became a chef whose promotional videotape bore the title "Barbecuing with Bobby." David Horowitz, a student radical during the 1960s and one-time editor of *Ramparts* magazine, became a Reagan Republican. Rennie Davis, a defendant in the celebrated Chicago conspiracy trial of 1969 resurfaced as a stockbroker. Actress Jane Fonda, denounced as "Hanoi Jane" during the Vietnam War, made a fortune producing exercise videos. Other

'60s radicals like Mark Rudd and Abby Hoffman emerged from hiding to live quiet lives or work peacefully for social change. None of these, however, really conformed to the yuppie profile.

The Wall Street Crash of October 19, 1987, ended the mystique surrounding young entrepreneurs. That day, as the dimension of the collapse expanded, anxious crowds gathered outside the New York Stock Exchange. A man began shouting, "The end is near! It's all over! The Reagan Revolution is over! Down with MBAs! Down with Yuppies!" Another member of the crowd tried to bolster confidence by yelling, "Whoever dies with the most toys wins!"

After only four years of grace, the term yuppie evolved into a slur. In 1988 *Newsweek* declared the group in "disgrace" and even suggested that the '80s were over, two years early. The *Wall Street Journal* reported "conspicuous consumption is passé." *New York* magazine, a purveyor to yuppie tastes, ran a cover story celebrating altruism and asked its readers: "HAD IT WITH PRIDE, COVETOUSNESS, LUST, ANGER, GLUTTONY, ENVY AND SLOTH? IT'S TIME TO START DOING GOOD."

The Other Americans

Far less glamorous than either the risk arbitrageurs of Wall Street or the yuppies of Los Angeles were the people of average income and the poor. Their experience during the 1980s differed markedly from the fables of wealth told by George Gilder. Measured in constant dollars, the average family income of the poorest fifth of the population dropped (from $5,439 to $4,107) while the income of the richest fifth swelled from $62,000 to $69,000. During the Reagan Recovery, the most affluent fifth of American households experienced a 14% increase in their wealth while the middle three-fifths experienced little or no improvement. Put simply, the rich got richer and everyone else tread water.

As a justification of his tax policy, President Reagan maintained that despite the cut in tax rates after 1981, federal revenues had grown. He neglected to mention that they never increased enough to cover the large expansion in military expenditures. But his assertion obscured the fact that the rate reductions favored the wealthy and that the total tax bite (which included Social Security, state, and sales taxes) paid by the average American family did not diminish and even increased slightly during the 1980s.

Economic growth after 1983 seemed impressive when compared to the late 1970s, but appeared less so when the base of comparison became the period from the Second World War through the Carter administration. Overall, the economy grew at a faster rate during the 1960s and 1970s than in the 1980s. Unemployment remained higher during the 1980s than in most years from 1947 to 1973. Real wages, which began to stagnate during the 1970s, continued to do so. In aggregate, individual salaries declined slightly during the Reagan years. The impact of this, however, was hidden because of a substantial increase in the number of working wives and mothers who boosted total family income. By 1989, the wealthiest two-fifths of American families received 67.8% of national income, while the bottom two-fifths earned a mere 15.4%—a larger spread than at any time since 1945.

Women and children were the most likely to be poor. The number of children living in poverty, one in five, had grown by 24% during the 1980s. The so-called feminization of poverty also grew more severe during the Reagan decade. The percentage of children living with a never married mother more than doubled during the 1980s, from 2.9 to 7%. By 1989 one of every four births in the United States was to an unwed woman. African-American and Hispanic women had the highest likelihood of becoming single mothers. Unwed mothers were less likely to receive prenatal care, finish high school, or hold a paying job.

These problems had complex causes and Reagan's policies were by no means responsible for creating them. But the refusal of his administration to address them seriously made the situation worse. In a particularly counterproductive move, the Reagan administration slashed spending for the WIC (Women-Infants-Children) program that provided pre- and post-natal care to poor women and helped reduce infant mortality rates and future medical costs.

Reagan defended reductions in social welfare spending with a typical quip. America, he remarked, had fought a war on poverty for nearly twenty years before he took office "and poverty won." At first glance, statistics he quoted seemed to confirm his dismal assessment. After an initial decline in the poverty rate to about

13% during the late Johnson and early Nixon administrations, the rate stalled at this level through the early 1980s.

But these aggregate numbers masked a major transformation in the nature of poverty. Increased spending on programs such as Social Security and Medicare dramatically improved the lot of the elderly and handicapped. They were much less likely to be poor by the 1980s than at any time since 1945. The bulk of the poor after 1980 consisted of single mothers, young children, and young minority men with little education and few job skills. These groups had either not been the beneficiaries of anti-poverty programs during the 1970s or were left in the lurch by spending cuts in such programs.

Rather than welfare spending "causing" dependency, as many conservatives argued, the surging rates of teen pregnancy, the breakdown of stable family structures in the minority community, and the loss of millions of basic manufacturing jobs in cities, where most of the poor now lived, contributed to the creation of the "new poor."

Supply-siders made much of the fact that the American economy produced 18 million jobs under Reagan. Yet, nearly as many jobs were created during the 1970s. The new jobs varied a good deal. About half paid $20,000 or more annually. Of the remainder, many paid minimum wage and were part-time only. Administration boosters blamed President Carter for the fact that between 1979 and 1984, some 11.5 million workers lost jobs because of plant closings. Deindustrialization in the so-called rust belt of the upper Midwest meant that laid-off skilled steel and auto workers often found replacement jobs paying much less than they earned previously.

Between 1981 and 1989, according to an estimate by the private Economic Policy Institute, the real hourly wage of the typical production worker had fallen by about 6% in terms of what it could buy in the marketplace. Young males with high school diplomas but no college had fared even worse, losing almost 20% of their purchasing power during the 1980s.

Both conservatives and liberals were troubled by the increasing size of a permanent homeless population and a seemingly unreachable urban "underclass." The underclass consisted largely of minorities, especially African-Americans. The homeless were divided among women and children fleeing abusive spouses, unskilled individuals with social problems, and the chronically mentally ill. Many lived on city streets, in parks, or in subway stations, begging for money and food. Reagan dismissed the problem by suggesting homeless people were either nuts or people who enjoyed their lifestyle. While true in some cases, it vastly oversimplified the problem. The President showed no interest in boosting support for community mental health programs that might aid the chronic mentally ill.

The specter of the homeless and urban underclass unsettled American sensibilities but had little affect on public policy. Conservatives saw poverty primarily as a personal failure. Government efforts to help only made matters worse and provided a disincentive for individual effort. Liberals believed government had a responsibility to help, but offered few suggestions beyond restoring funds cut from social service programs.

Conservative Justice

In July 1987, when President Reagan nominated Judge Robert H. Bork to fill a vacant seat on the Supreme Court, leaders of the New Right were ecstatic. "Conservatives have waited over thirty years for this day," commented Richard Viguerie, a leading fund raiser for conservative causes. Viguerie predicted that Bork would become part of an emerging high court majority prepared to reverse many of the civil rights and civil liberties decisions made since 1954.

Discontent with the direction of Supreme Court rulings had spread beyond the New Right. Many ordinary citizens and state legislators complained that concern for defendants' rights had superseded the value of protecting law-abiding citizens. During the 1980s state legislatures as well as Congress mandated longer, compulsory prison sentences for many crimes. Jail and prison populations swelled by nearly 100% while prison construction and maintenance costs became the fastest growing category in state budgets. By 1989, just over a million Americans, nearly one for every 250 citizens, were in jail or prison, either awaiting trial or serving time. Over 90% of these were in state or local institutions and the remainder under federal detention. The United States led the world in its rate of incarceration. Only South Africa and the Soviet Union came close.

Since his days as governor of California, Reagan had criticized judges for putting too much value on individual liberties and protecting the rights of defendants to the detriment of police power and victims of crime. He echoed the charge of religious conservatives that liberal judges had "driven God out of the classroom" by banning prayer in public schools while condoning pre-marital sex, homosexuality, and a disrespect for authority. Like many conservatives, Reagan held the somewhat contradictory belief that courts should limit public regulation of the economy while allowing government to regulate private morality, sexual behavior, and reproductive rights.

Attorneys General William French Smith and his successor, Edwin Meese, III, insisted that Supreme Court decisions should be based exclusively on the "original meaning of the Constitution." This alone provided the "only reliable guide for judgment." In their view, since the Constitution was silent on issues such as abortion, privacy rights, contraception, artistic expression, and affirmative action, liberal justices had erred in extending constitutional protection for such things.

As president, Reagan promised to select judges concerned with "protecting the rights of law-abiding citizens," defending "traditional values and the sanctity of human life," and who endorsed "judicial restraint." Instead of judges making the law, they would be limited to interpreting it while "decision-making power [reverted] to state and local elected officials."

But Reagan faced a dilemma since neither Congress nor most state legislatures showed much interest in enacting his "social agenda" into law. Thus, the administration hoped conservative judges would, in effect, implement part of the agenda. Through a careful, highly political, winnowing process, Justice Department screening panels identified judicial nominees who agreed to interpret the Constitution to permit restrictions upon abortion, allow voluntary school prayer and government assistance to parochial schools, disallow affirmative action, and grant police greater authority to interrogate suspects and use illegally seized evidence in court. The president

Swearing in of Sandra Day O'Connor as Associate Justice of the Supreme Court. *Courtesy U.S. National Archives.*

had no qualms about "judicial activism" so long as its purpose was to rescind previous liberal decisions and to impose standards of moral behavior that elected representatives refused to do.

Normal attrition and the creation of 85 new federal judgeships permitted Reagan to appoint almost 400 federal judges—a majority of all those sitting in 1989. In addition, he had the opportunity to select a chief justice of the Supreme Court and three associate justices.

The president's first three Supreme Court appointments—Sandra Day O'Connor and Antonin Scalia as associate justices and William Rehnquist promoted from associate to chief justice—were confirmed by the Senate without much dissent. Although all were quite conservative, they were clearly qualified appointments. The Senate, with a Democratic majority restored in January 1987, rejected Robert Bork's 1987 nomination to the high court. It did so as much because of Bork's abrasive personality and his role in President Richard Nixon's firing of special prosecutor Archibald Cox during Watergate as his conservative philosophy. Bork's contention that the Constitution offered little protection for privacy, free speech, women, and minorities angered many senators. Judge Anthony Kennedy, whose successful nomination followed Bork's defeat, shared many of Bork's views but did not antagonize people in the same way.

Only after Kennedy's confirmation, late in 1988, did the Reagan appointees, along with associate justice Bryon White, form a de facto conservative majority on many issues. Justice Scalia appeared to be the most activist conservative on the bench, voting to overturn many liberal precedents on such issues as abortion, school prayer, free speech, affirmative action, and rights to privacy.

Reagan's Justice Department took an especially dim view of enforcing civil rights legislation during the 1980s. The president had opposed most of the civil rights acts passed since the 1960s and supported a constitutional amendment to outlaw school busing. Early in his presidency he criticized Martin Luther King, Jr., as immoral, tainted by communist affiliation, and someone who should not be honored with a federal holiday. When Congress enacted such a holiday in 1983, Reagan signed the law with great fanfare and spoke eloquently about King's contribution to American justice.

This did not change administration policy. Shortly after taking office, Reagan outraged civil rights groups by ordering the Justice Department to argue before the Supreme Court that tax benefits be restored to segregated private schools and colleges. (The IRS had stripped such schools of their preferred tax status.) In 1983 the high court rebuffed the administration and ruled that the IRS had acted properly in denying tax benefits.

The Justice Department attacked affirmative action programs—preferential hiring plans designed to offset the legacy of discrimination—as a "racial spoils system." Until 1988, a majority of Supreme Court justices voted to uphold many affirmative action plans. But following the confirmation of Justice Kennedy, a majority of the justices voted in a series of cases during 1989 (the most important of which was *City of Richmond* v. *J.A. Corson, Co.*) to forbid as reverse discrimination government or private employers from setting aside a quota of jobs or contracts for minorities. In five related decisions, the justices made it more difficult for women, the elderly, and minorities to sue employers accused of job discrimination.

Administration hostility toward civil rights was frequently expressed by the conscious maladministration of law by executive agencies. For example, Clarence Thomas, whom President George Bush appointed to the Supreme Court in 1991, served as director of civil rights in the U.S. Department of Education and as chairman of the Equal Employment Opportunity Commission under Reagan. While in the Education Department he acknowledged in a court hearing that he was violating court-ordered deadlines for processing complaints of discrimination in higher education because they ran counter to the administration's philosophy. As EEOC chair, he permitted age-discrimination claims by thousands of older workers to lapse without action and declined to press many class-action discrimination suits because he objected to the principle of class-action suits.

Further evidence of hostility toward racial minorities emerged when the Reagan administration urged Congress not to renew the landmark 1965 Voting Rights Act that assured African-Americans in the South federal protection in registering and voting. When Congress renewed the law anyway, the Justice Department declined to investigate many allegations of interference with voting rights. Instead, officials made a special effort to investigate possible fraud in voter registration projects, especially those that succeeded in electing blacks to office.

The president and his two attorneys general convinced many Americans that what they called "constitutional loopholes and technicalities" should not frustrate the enforcement efforts of police and prosecutors. Attorney General Meese called the American Civil Liberties Union a "criminal's lobby" and declared that "if a person is innocent of a crime, then he is not a suspect." Reagan's appointees to the Supreme Court voted consistently to expand police power and limit protection extended to criminal defendants. After 1984, the Supreme Court affirmed most state death penalty laws, approved denying bail in some cases, whittled away at police responsibility to alert suspects of their right to remain silent, and ruled that prosecutors could introduce in court some illegally seized evidence if the police, during a search, acted in "good faith."

Private Spheres and Public Policies

Throughout his presidency, Ronald Reagan spoke out strongly on a number of moral issues, including abortion, drug use, prayer in school, sexuality, and the importance of traditional family values. At the same time, Reagan avoided expending very much political capital in pursuit of these controversial goals. For example, he addressed the annual "pro-life," anti-abortion rally in Washington by telephone, making certain that he would not be photographed alongside the strident movement leaders. Reagan worked hard to keep social conservatives in his corner but avoided political confrontations with Congress.

Just Say No

American presidents, starting with Woodrow Wilson, have declared a series of wars on drugs. The federal role began with the passage of the Harrison Act in 1916, which banned opiates and classified drug users as criminals. A New Deal law of 1937 made marijuana use a federal crime. Laws passed during the Truman, Eisenhower, and Nixon administrations broadened the penalties against drug use and criminalized a wider variety of natural and synthetic substances. Nixon replaced the Narcotics Bureau with a more powerful Drug Enforcement Administration, and Reagan bolstered the DEA further. Narcotics laws sent many people to jail but had little impact on the problem. The use of opiates, marijuana, and other psychoactive drugs waxed and waned in a rhythm of its own.

The American approach to drug control had long relied on three weapons: (1) the eradication of opium poppies, marijuana, and coca leaf at its foreign source (Turkey, Peru, Southeast Asia, for example); (2) the interdiction of drugs as they entered the United States; and (3) vigorous police efforts to arrest drug dealers and users in the local community. Ever since 1916 these efforts had been highly politicized and dismal failures.

Historically, drug-use patterns are difficult to predict or understand. However, in many cases the use of psychoactive substances such as heroin, marijuana, and cocaine have tended to run in cycles. A new drug is introduced, finds a following, experiences a surge in use for five to ten years, and then declines in popularity when the user community sees its dangerous effects. During the 1950s heroin use rose and declined, marijuana was in vogue from the middle 1960s through the late 1970s, and cocaine use escalated during the second half of the 1970s. This generalization must also take into account varying levels of drug use among different economic classes and ethnic and minority groups.

In 1985, 1% of Americans surveyed listed drugs as a major threat to the nation. By 1989, more than half the population described drug use as a grave threat to national security. President and Mrs. Reagan, declaring that the nation faced an unprecedented epidemic of drug use, urged even stricter criminal penalties and implored the public to "just say no." When Reagan left office, federal, state, and local authorities were spending about $15 billion annually to fight a "war on drugs." Three-fourths of the money went to law enforcement and incarceration. Drug offenders constituted the fastest growing sector of the prison population.

The Reagan anti-drug crusade coincided with the reduction of tension with the Soviet Union during the president's second term. To an extent, the drug war replaced the Cold War while "narco-terrorism" replaced the Red Army as public enemy #1. This "militarization" of drug policy found expression in a National Security Council directive Reagan approved in 1986, calling drug traffic a threat to the security of the United States and the entire Western hemisphere. Just as the Chinese Communists had been blamed during the 1950s for the surge in heroin addiction, Reagan accused communist governments in Cuba and Nicaragua of abetting cocaine imports. As we will see, he conveniently overlooked involvement by anti-communist guerrillas in Latin American drug trafficking.

The public tended to ignore the foreign policy implications of the Reagan anti-drug campaign but did respond to individual tragedy. The 1986 death from cocaine overdose of Len Bias, a promising basketball player at the University of Maryland who had just signed a lucrative professional contract, became a major national news event. Journalists and public officials asked, plaintively, why an athlete with such promise used cocaine. Few questioned how he had reached his senior year despite failing most of his courses.

Ronald and Nancy Reagan denounced drug use as immoral and reaffirmed their belief that religion, school discipline, and harsh criminal penalties were the best antidote. Whether true or not, the Reagan's definition of norms varied dramatically from the real behavior of Americans. Each year during the 1980s, an estimated 40 million people (about one in six) consumed an illegal substance. A 1987 survey revealed that half of all citizens under age 45 had smoked marijuana at least once in their life. Almost three-quarters of a million Americans faced drug charges each year in the 1980s, mostly for possession of marijuana.

In spite of the hysteria about increasing drug use, accurate statistics were hard to come by. Local police stepped up enforcement of narcotic laws when the issue gained prominence. Police departments also learned that they could secure larger budgets by stressing the drug problem. Impartial experts believe that drug use among non-minorities and the middle class probably peaked at the end of the 1970s and actually declined during the 1980s.

In contrast, use of cocaine and its derivatives, like crack, grew in popularity among the urban poor and minority youth. For some, staying high relieved the miseries of daily life. Others found selling drugs provided one of the few avenues of economic and social mobility. The effects on individual, family, and community life were tragic. But the response of government at all levels—putting more drug users in jail—basically ignored the tragedy. While the social stigma and physical trauma of mandatory jail time probably deterred many middle-class youth from using drugs, it had little impact on inner-city minorities who often found a year or two of incarceration an improvement on their normal living conditions.

The federal government and media seldom discussed the root causes of drug use and often misrepresented its physical consequences. Narcotics killed relatively few drug users—about 4,000 to 5,000 in a typical year during the 1980s. America's legal drugs of choice—alcohol and tobacco—killed 200 to 300 times as many people. For example, alcohol-related deaths approached 200,000 annually while tobacco killed over 300,000 Americans each year.

Violent turf wars among drug dealers and robberies to raise money for drug buys killed twice as many people—about 8,000 annually—as narcotics did directly.

Nancy Reagan first visited a crisis nursery for children of drug addicts in 1984. She delivered a speech written by Peggy Noonan, whom she had neither met nor discussed the subject with. "The things I've seen," she told reporters (in Noonan's words), "would make the strongest heart break." She and the president repeated these visits several times over the next four years.

President Reagan, like most citizens, was more troubled by the escalation of drug-related violence than with the question of why youths used drugs or how to rehabilitate addicts. The aggressive behavior associated with smoking "crack" cocaine seemed especially worrisome. The Drug Enforcement Agency focused anti-drug efforts on the dramatic but largely futile campaign to interdict supplies, arrest dealers, and jail users. For example, Reagan placed Vice President George Bush in charge of a task force to halt drug smuggling into Florida. Predictably, less drugs entered Florida, as smugglers shifted operations elsewhere.

The Drug Enforcement Administration and local authorities measured success in the tonnage of drugs seized and the numbers of smugglers arrested. Since the cost of producing and transporting drugs represented a small portion of eventual profits, interdiction hardly made a dent in the incentive to smuggle. Perhaps because therapy programs were much less telegenic than car and boat chases, only about one-fourth of the money expended on the drug problem and little attention went into drug education or rehabilitation.

In his enthusiasm to suppress drugs, President Reagan urged compulsory urine tests—chemical loyalty oaths, as civil libertarians called them—of millions of workers who showed no evidence of abuse. In many cases, courts permitted this. By 1989, state and federal prisons were bursting with drug felons sentenced to long mandatory terms but cocaine was as available as before. Police began reporting decreased levels of cocaine use in 1990. Predictably, authorities claimed success. However, as with earlier drug epidemics, the "consumer product cycle," rather than legal sanctions, played a large role. Many addicts and casual users seemed to have switched brands, often to a new generation of synthetic drugs or to an old standby, heroin. Polling data suggested that the public had begun turning its attention in other directions. In any case, during the 1980s, as before, alcohol remained the drug most abused by all sectors of American society.[1]

A Nation at Risk

Several times this century, some influential group of Americans has warned of a crisis in public education. For example, following the Soviet launch of the Sputnik satellite in 1957, journalists, scientists, politicians, and parents worried that the "superior" Soviet school system had won the "brain race" as well as the space race. "What would the first American on the moon find?" ran a joke of the time: "Russians," came the somber answer. The scare mobilized Congress and the Eisenhower administration into supporting the landmark National Defense Education Act. Like the GI Bill a decade before, this infusion of tax dollars revitalized public education and helped make the United States the world's center of higher education during the following decades.

By the 1980s, the Soviets were no longer the bogeyman of American education. Fear now centered on stories about high schools turning out illiterates while Japanese students routinely outperformed Americans on standardized tests. A response came from an unlikely source: Reagan's Secretary of Education, Terrel Bell.

Bell had served as Commissioner of Education during the Nixon administration. Reagan's talent scouts thought that as a conservative Mormon from Utah, Bell would be an Education Secretary supportive of the administration's goal of abolishing the recently created cabinet department. They were so certain of this they never bothered to ask the appointee his views. Bell, in fact, was an honorable man, committed to the principle of federal financial support for the nation's public education system. At the first Cabinet meet-

[1] The anti-drug crusade of the 1980s coincided with other "abstinence" movements. Advocates of natural foods denounced the "deadly white powders," meaning salt and sugar. Groups such as Mothers Against Drunk Driving (MADD) campaigned to stiffen state laws against drunk drivers. Anti-tobacco advocates pressed local government to mandate smoke-free work places and restaurants. Breweries could barely produce enough "light" beer to slake the nation's thirst.

ing he attended in 1981, Bell was suspected of not being a team player when he declined to eat jelly beans from the jar the president passed around the table.

Bell grew frustrated and angry with pressure from the White House to enforce selectively anti-discrimination laws and to join in the chorus supporting reduction in the level of aid to schools. In an adroit bureaucratic move, the Education Secretary convened a blue-ribbon panel to assess the condition of American education. The resulting 1983 study, "A Nation at Risk: The Imperative for National Reform," reported that "if an unfriendly foreign power had attempted to impose on America the mediocre educational performance that exists today, we might well have viewed it as an act of war."

Americans generally sympathized with the tone of the report, but few agreed on a remedy. Conservatives blamed permissive teachers, sex education, wasteful spending, and a lack of attention to Western cultural traditions and the basic "3 R's" for poor outcomes. Liberals complained that the public schools were underfunded and hard pressed to teach both traditional subjects and the high tech skills needed in a competitive world.

Public schools faced two problems that defied ideological categories: an aging population that resented school taxes and a growing concentration of poor and minority pupils. As the overall population aged, a larger proportion of voters opposed raising taxes to pay for something they felt had little benefit to them. Meanwhile, a growing portion of the affluent middle class, especially in cities, abandoned public schools. They enrolled their children in private and parochial schools that had selective admission policies. The departure of many of the more motivated students left public schools to educate a larger proportion of poor, minority, or otherwise disadvantaged children. Middle-class flight further reduced school districts' ability to raise needed revenues. Parents who opted for private and parochial education were reluctant to support new school taxes. Working-class parents had less faith in the value of education and saw school tax increases as just another financial burden. These divisions accentuated the decline of faith in public education and deprived the younger generations of a common, shaping experience.

Secretary of Education Terrel Bell's fate under Reagan revealed the administration's priorities. The president endorsed Bell's 1983 report and tapped the Education Secretary to appear alongside him during the 1984 re-election campaign. But soon after the election, Bell was summarily fired. His successor, William Bennett, muted calls for increased federal funding for public schools and emphasized, instead, discipline and teaching traditional morality.

Religion and Public Life

The influence of politically active fundamentalists and evangelical Christians continued well into the Reagan administration. Religious broadcasters prospered as never before. By 1985, the combined take of several hundred electronic ministries totaled well over $1 billion annually. Donations from viewers supported a variety of religious, charitable, political, and business causes, often funneled through unregulated funds such as the Moral Majority, the 700 Club, and the PTL ministry.

Televangelists preached at least two sermons. One fulminated against the threat posed by immorality, communism, abortion, and "secular humanism," a belief that humans, not God, were the basis for morality. The other celebrated a "gospel of wealth." Rev. Jimmy Swaggart epitomized the former style and Rev. Jim Bakker the latter. Both promised grace and a place in heaven via generous donations while here on earth.

Hellfire-and-brimstone preachers, along with the "feel good" variety, tapped into major trends in the 1980s. President Reagan's campaign against Godless communism and the Soviet Union's evil empire (discussed below) resembled Jimmy Swaggart's talk of sin and Satan. Jim and Tammy Faye Bakker's PTL show celebrated wealth and conspicuous consumption as a form of divine grace. The Bakkers told their viewers words to the effect "you can't do good unto others unless you feel good about yourself, and you can't feel good about yourself unless you have a lot of neat stuff." Tammy Faye practiced what she preached. For husband Jim's televised birthday party, she gave him a present of two live giraffes. On another show, Tammy had Jim preside over a wedding for two pet dogs.

Assessing the influence of the electronic ministries is difficult. Not all, or even most, televangelists were flimflam artists. Nor did all viewers accept the political doctrines put forth by media preachers. Many who watched the shows simply enjoyed the hymns, entertainment, and patriotic symbolism. Even a large number of donors, pollsters reported, contributed money out of a sense of responsibility to pay for watching the spectacle, just as those watching public TV gave during "pledge week."

Several of the most powerful televangelists fell from grace during 1987, while President Reagan became deeply embroiled in the Iran-Contra scandal. Money and sex proved their undoing. Federal prosecutors indicted Jim Bakker on numerous counts of fraud and conspiracy for bilking followers who invested $158 million in a combined hotel and religious theme park called Heritage USA and for stealing some $3 million in ministry funds. In essence, PTL operated as a pyramid scheme. Around the same time, a rival TV preacher revealed that Bakker had forced a female church member, Jessica Hahn, to have sex with him and used donations to pay her over $200,000 in hush money.

Bakker resigned from PTL, blaming his troubles on rival Jimmy Swaggart who, he charged lusted after the PTL theme park. Hahn, interviewed for a nude *Penthouse* magazine feature, explained that Bakker forced her to have sex by saying, "When you help the shepherd, you help the sheep." A jury convicted Bakker of cheating investors and he received a stiff jail term. The *Charlotte Observer*, whose reporters won a Pulitzer Prize for their exposure of Bakker's scheme, remarked in an editorial that it was fine for a preacher to promise his flock eternal life in a celestial city, "but if he promises an annual free stay in a luxury hotel here on earth, he'd better have the rooms available."

The revelations about popular media preachers came to resemble a soap opera. Jimmy Swaggart, Bakker's nemesis, was fingered by one of his rivals for frequenting prostitutes. After one prostitute described Swaggart as "really kinky," the minister made a tearful, televised confession. Faith healer Oral Roberts became an object of derision when he locked himself in a prayer tower claiming that "God would take him away" unless his flock mailed him several million dollars in a few weeks. Roberts' salvation came when a gambler made a large contribution. Reverend Pat Robertson, who controlled the large and profitable Christian Broadcasting Network, saw his campaign for the Republican presidential nomination collapse amidst laughter after he described how his prayers had diverted a hurricane from Virginia Beach to the more Godless New York City. Jerry Falwell, though not tainted by scandal, quit the Moral Majority in 1988 and devoted himself to church activities.

President Reagan distanced himself from the media preachers in time to avoid any direct taint. The so-called Gospel-Gate scandals came as little surprise to journalists covering the electronic church. Personal and financial lapses among certain televangelists had long been rumored. The Internal Revenue Service, Federal Communications Commission, and Justice Department had sought to investigate evidence of fraud and tax evasion but were pressed not to do so by the White House, which saw the Bakkers, Swaggart, and other media preachers as important allies. As historian Frances Fitzgerald observed, the televangelist empire, like Reagan's trust in the Laffer Curve, was built largely on faith and not-quite-innocent belief in miracles.

Sex and Gender in the 1980s

Through their public pronouncements and support for new laws, Ronald and Nancy Reagan attempted to alter the sexual behavior of many Americans and their attitudes toward abortion and the rights of women. During the 1980s, fear of sexually transmitted disease, bolstered by conservative opposition to abortion and the Equal Rights Amendment, dominated discussion of sex and gender issues. President Reagan, who condemned abortion as murder, urged pre-marital chastity and championed the "traditional" family of husband as breadwinner, wife as mother and homemaker. Conservatives predicted that the decade would assure the "end of the sexual revolution."

The president's words, critics charged, rang false. Reagan was the first divorced man elected president and had married two career women. He had a distant relationship with his children, two of whom, Patti and Michael, had written books that criticized their parents as hypocrites. Reagan's personal life aside, the traditional family he celebrated was an endangered specie. The number of households composed of a married couple and one or more children under age 18 had declined steadily over recent decades. In 1970, 40% of the nation's households mirrored this ideal. By 1980, only 31% did. Barely a fourth of households were "traditional" as of 1991.

Reagan won plaudits for appointing a few women to high-profile positions during his first term. These included Jeane Kirkpatrick as ambassador to the United Nations, Margaret Heckler to head the Health and Human Services Department, and Sandra Day O'Connor as the first female associate justice of the Supreme Court. Overall, however, Reagan appointed fewer women to influential jobs than his three predecessors.

Feminists raised other concerns about private and public policies relating to gender. They decried women's lack of access to well-paying jobs, affordable child care, and reproductive freedom. They noted the growing number of women and young children living in poverty. Under Reagan, government either ignored these problems or took actions that made them worse.

The public debate over appropriate sexuality was complicated by the appearance of AIDS (acquired immune deficiency syndrome) in the early 1980s. A disease thought to have originated in Africa, the AIDS virus destroyed victims' immune systems and left them vulnerable to opportunistic infections. After much confusion, doctors determined that the main source of infection was through bodily fluids, such as semen and blood. Male homosexuals, intravenous drug users, and hemophiliacs faced the greatest risk of infection. As of 1991, the disease had killed over 100,000 Americans. Health experts predicted that over 200,000 victims would die by the end of 1993. In Africa, AIDS struck even harder.

Before 1985, Reagan all but ignored the epidemic. Although he had homosexual friends from his days in Hollywood, the president seemed uneasy discussing the disease, its mode of transmission, or preventive measures. The president appeared to find the entire subject distasteful and felt that anything he said expressing a sympathetic attitude toward its victims might upset religious conservatives who called the illness divine punishment of sinners. Among his own staff, this attitude was forcefully expressed by Patrick Buchanan who wrote: "The poor homosexuals. They have declared war on nature and now nature is exacting an awful retribution."

Scientists, including Surgeon General Dr. C. Everett Koop, urged public officials to endorse a "safe sex" program, since use of condoms reduced transmission of the virus. Fundamentalists, as well as the president, took "safe sex" to mean "no sex." During his first term, Reagan avoided discussing the AIDS problem, opposed spending much federal money on research, and exercised no leadership.

The president's attitude began to change after October 1985 when actor and matinee idol Rock Hudson died of the disease. He was a friend of the Reagans and his death humanized AIDS for the first family and many ordinary Americans. By early 1986, the president called AIDS research a top priority (though he still resisted spending additional money to study it) and asked the Surgeon General to prepare a report on the affliction.

Koop's recommendations, issued in October 1986, called on Americans to change their personal behavior. He described his remedy as "one, abstinence; two, monogamy; three, condoms." Conservatives such as Jerry Falwell, Phyllis Schlafly, and Education Secretary William Bennett condemned Koop for encouraging immorality by stressing the need for sexually active people to use condoms. The Surgeon General urged Reagan to take the lead in telling Americans more about the disease and how to prevent it. But the President shied away from personal involvement with this public health crisis. In his one major speech on AIDS, in May 1987, he merely said that scientists were "still learning about how AIDS is transmitted" and that the public should not be afraid to donate blood. He never mentioned sex or condoms.

Reagan imposed his conservative sexual mores on other public issues. He persuaded Congress to bar most public funding for birth control and stop Medicare from funding abortions for poor women. An administration measure provided funding for religiously oriented "chastity clinics" where counselors advised teenage girls and women to "just say no" to avoid pregnancy.

As noted earlier, Reagan endorsed the so-called Right to Life movement and supported a constitutional amendment barring abortion except to save the life of a mother. At least one member of the president's inner circle had a unique perspective on the subject. Shortly before the president left office, Peter Grace, who chaired the Grace Commission to recommend efficiency in government, introduced Reagan at a banquet of anti-abortion advocates. It took a man like Reagan, Grace explained, to point out the simple truth that "all living people started life as feces." When some listeners gasped, Grace repeated himself forcefully: "Yes, even you started out as feces. And now dinner is served."

Reagan, like many conservatives, pursued the goal of recoupling sex and reproduction, two activities which since the 1960s had been decoupled. Women's access to abortion and contraception, like gay sex, defied the linkage of sex, reproduction, and marriage. Despite the president's effort to affect public opinion, at the end of his term a strong majority of Americans continued to favor the right of a woman to choose abortion.

The generally more conservative public view toward gender issues did permit Republican members of Congress in 1982 to block reconsideration of the Equal Rights Amendment to the Constitution when its deadline for approval lapsed. Reagan also succeeded in blocking congressional efforts to develop a national child-care policy, even though a majority of women with young children had entered the workforce.

Although Reagan failed to persuade Congress to pass a constitutional amendment banning abortion, he selected Supreme Court justices who, he hoped, would eventually form a majority voting to strike down constitutional protection for abortion and privacy rights. In something of an irony, the president who advocated "judicial restraint" relied on activist judges to implement his social agenda.

The New Immigration and Ethnicity

The expanding rate, and changing pattern, of immigration proved one of the most dramatic social changes of the 1980s. Starting with the Immigration Act of 1965, which dropped ethnic quotas, first a trickle, then a river, of non-Europeans came to the United States.

Between the mid-1970s and 1990, over a half million people migrated to this country each year, 90% of them from Asia, the Middle East, the Caribbean, or Latin America.

In his speech accepting the Republican presidential nomination in August 1980, Ronald Reagan described America as an "island of freedom." He asked the convention delegates to join him in thanking "Divine Providence" for making this nation a haven for refugees fleeing oppression and disaster. At the end of his presidency, he repeated this theme. In his January 1989 Farewell Address, Reagan cited a letter from a sailor aboard the aircraft carrier *Midway*, in the South China Sea. The crew saw a refugee-laden boat in danger of sinking. Risking their own lives, a rescue party set out in a small launch to help. As one of the *Midway*'s seaman stepped aboard, an Indochinese refugee "stood up and called out to him 'Hello American sailor, Hello Freedom Man.' " This incident, Reagan explained, symbolized America's promise to the world.

Reagan's vintage inspirational anecdote did not reflect his administration's attitude toward many immigrants and refugees. For example, shortly after taking office in 1981, he ordered the Coast Guard to tow out to sea any boats of Haitian refugees found approaching America. For these unfortunate souls, American sailors were not "Freedom Men."

In 1989, among 248 million residents of the United States, there were about 31 million African-Americans, 22 million Hispanics, and 7 million Asians. Since the 1970s, nearly 45% of documented immigrants came from Asia and the Middle East, about as many from Latin America and the Caribbean, and just over 10% from Europe. The Hispanic population grew by over 50% during the 1980s. The pace of Asian immigration was even more dramatic. The arrival of 3.5 million Filipinos, Chinese, Koreans, and Vietnamese doubled the number of Asian-Americans within ten years. While many Indochinese came as "boat people" fleeing oppression, most Asian immigrants were well educated and many had family members living in this country.

As in earlier periods, immigrants worked hard and filled vital niches in the economy. For example, in New York City, recently arrived Asians and Hispanics virtually rescued the garment industry from a labor shortage. Many immigrants opened small neighborhood stores. Foreign-born nurses, orderlies, and doctors made up nearly half the staff in the nation's public hospitals.

Higher than average birth rates among Hispanics, Asians, and African-Americans, along with immigration, led demographers to predict that by the middle of the next century a majority of the American population would trace its roots to non-European cultures. California set the pace of change. By 1989, nearly one in eight Americans, some 30 million people, lived there. Hispanics and Asians composed 80% of the population added to the state since 1980. By 1991, Hispanics made up one-fourth of the state's residents, Asians a tenth.

Two major laws passed during the 1980s regulated the entry of refugees and immigrants. At the end of the Carter administration, Congress enacted the Refugee Act of 1980 designed to protect those in flight because of a "well-founded fear of persecution" for religious, political, or racial reasons. The law represented an effort to treat refugees from all countries equally. However, the Reagan administration implemented it selectively. Nearly anyone fleeing Cuba or Nicaragua received political asylum, while most Salvadorans, Haitians, and Guatemalans, whose regimes Washington counted as allies, were labeled inadmissable "economic" refugees.

Some Americans considered this selective refugee policy a violation of both law and morality. A small group formed a "Sanctuary Movement" modeled on the Underground Railroad to help those fleeing oppression. These activists organized a network of churches and other institutions to shelter refugees who would otherwise be sent home. Boston and Cambridge declared themselves "sanctuary cities" and in Tucson, Arizona, local ministers and concerned citizens crossed the border with Mexico to transport Central Americans denied legal entry into the United States.

The Immigration and Naturalization Service and Justice Department took a dim view of these actions. They denied favoring refugees of one nationality over another and labeled sanctuary workers "alien smugglers." Federal agents infiltrated the Sanctuary Movement and won convictions of several leaders in federal trials.

The pace and nature of the new immigration aroused mixed feelings among the general public. African-Americans resented what they saw as favored treatment accorded new arrivals. Some whites complained that English had become a second language in parts of the country. Concerned citizens in California, Arizona, and Florida passed laws declaring English the official state language and forbade state employees to conduct business in other tongues.

The presence of undocumented Mexicans living in the United States, whose number might be anywhere from 3 to 15 million, aroused special concern. After years of debate on how to control immigration, Congress in 1986 passed the Simpson-Rodino Law. It offered legal status to undocumented aliens who had lived and worked in the United States for some time but imposed fines on employers who hired new undocumented workers. Hispanics and Asian-Americans feared this would discourage employers from hiring them. The impact of these provisions on illegal immigration is unclear. In any case, during 1989 nearly one million people migrated to the United States, a number not seen since before World War I.

As in other spheres, Reagan era policy toward immigration affected events only at the margins. The President's tax and spending initiatives did not alter the economic situation of most Americans. The conservative social agenda generated controversy without changing personal behavior. The appointment of conservative judges at all levels of the federal judiciary will probably have the most lasting impact on issues of privacy, civil rights, and civil liberties. Reagan's crusade to eliminate regulation of the economy, as we shall see, generated some of the most dramatic, if unintended, results of his presidency.

4

Prophets (Profits) of De-regulation

S INCE THE 1950s, Ronald Reagan had criticized government efforts to regulate the private economy. Not just prosperity, he declared, but "fundamental freedoms were in jeopardy because of the emergence of a *permanent government* . . . a federal bureaucracy . . . so powerful it was able to set policy and thwart the desires of not only ordinary citizens" but of elected representatives as well. In his first economic message to Congress, the president decried "waste and fraud" in government and gross mismanagement by federal regulators. Government oversight and hostility toward the private sector, he believed, had stifled the creativity of American business.

The de-regulation movement began seriously during the Carter administration, pushed forward by President Carter and a coalition of Democratic liberals, Republican conservatives, and academic specialists at the University of Chicago and Cornell University. They targeted regulations that limited competition and kept prices high in the trucking, railroad, airline, and telephone industries. Consumers generally applauded the de-regulation of these industries since prices came down and service often improved.

Unlike the first generation of regulatory relief proponents, Reagan and his advisers made little distinction between removing anticompetitive barriers and dumping wholesale the provisions protecting worker health and safety and the environment. The new administration championed all de-regulation as "getting government off the backs of the people." The Office of Management and Budget, the Commerce Department, a presidential commission chaired by businessman Peter Grace, and a task force headed by Vice President George Bush drew up plans to eliminate hundreds of rules, including those affecting disposal of hazardous waste, air pollution, nuclear safety, and exposure to chemicals. The meat-ax, pro-business effort at de-regulation proved counterproductive in the long run, as it aroused opposition from Congress, the public, and federal courts.

Proponents of wide-ranging de-regulation and privatization in the Reagan administration believed the policy made political and practical sense. Officials such as Interior Secretary James Watt and Environmental Protection Administration (EPA) official Anne Gorsuch Burford were ideologically, and in Watt's case religiously, opposed to most government-mandated efforts to protect the natural environment. "We will mine more, drill more, cut more timber," the Interior Secretary boasted upon taking office in 1981. As Mark S. Fowler, the lawyer Reagan appointed to head the Federal Communications Commission, responded to those who wanted the FCC to regulate more carefully the broadcast industry: "Television is just another appliance. It's a toaster with pictures." Ed Gray, Reagan's choice to supervise the de-regulation of the Savings and Loan industry later remarked, "the administration was so ideologically blinded that it couldn't understand the difference between" lowering airfares and removing all controls from part of the banking system.

The Ideological Crusaders

James G. Watt, a lawyer from Colorado, emerged as the New Right's star among the Reagan Cabinet. A hardline conservative and born-again Christian, Watt had the influential backing of Colorado beer baron and Reagan-crony, Joseph Coors. Two kinds of people lived in this country, Watt once explained: "Liberals and Americans." In the late 1970s he founded, with Coors' financial help, the Mountain States Legal Foundation dedicated to fighting environmental groups (such as the "charity mob" in the Audubon

Society) and government agencies that limited economic development on public lands. To Watt and his fellow activists, the American West represented a storehouse of mineral wealth, not nature's treasury. Reagan's election seemed a divine sign that the federal government would open more coastal waters to oil drilling and additional public lands to mining and logging.

Watt spoke forcefully on many New Right issues. He once commented that "as a white man I will be very hesitant to allow a black doctor to operate on me because I will always have the feeling that he may have been carried by the quota system." When asked how he intended to fulfill his pledge to manage and preserve the public lands, the Interior Secretary observed that his stewardship would be guided by the "scriptures which call upon us to occupy the land until Jesus returns." Watt, one journalist quipped, interpreted biblical phrases about "subduing the earth" to mean "God created the earth just for Mobil Oil."

As Interior Secretary, Watt purged the department of many career employees he considered anti-growth or pro-environment. He altered offshore leasing procedures so that oil companies, rather than Interior Department specialists, could determine which tracts should be auctioned for exploration. At one point, he opened for drilling the coastal waters off California's Big Sur. Deciding for himself that sufficient recreational land existed, Watt ordered the Interior Department to stop acquiring new acreage for national parks.

Reagan usually avoided the intense controversy sparked by Watt, even though he considered the Interior Secretary a useful ally. Watt proved a mesmerizing speaker in front of conservative audiences and raised large amounts of money for Republican causes. When pragmatists like James Baker complained about Watt's extremism, the Interior Secretary insisted that he had the president's full confidence and publicly called on the White House moderates to "Let Reagan be Reagan."

Watt's tastes in culture and humor, rather than his cavalier handling of public resources, proved his undoing. In July 1982 he cancelled a concert by the popular Beach Boys, scheduled as part of the Fourth of July celebration on the Capital Mall. He claimed that the aging surfer singers projected a bad image and should not perform on public property. In their place, he selected Wayne

Newton, a Las Vegas lounge entertainer. Unbeknownst to Watt, Nancy Reagan had a special fondness for the Beach Boys and joined those urging the president to find a new Interior Secretary.

Watt succumbed to foot-in-mouth disease in September 1983. Pressured into naming a public advisory panel to oversee a coal-leasing venture, the Interior Secretary sarcastically told a breakfast gathering of the U.S. Chamber of Commerce he had selected a balanced group. "We have every kind of mix you can have. I have a black, I have a woman, two Jews and a cripple." In one quip, he had offended a record number of Americans. With the Senate set to vote on a resolution condemning him and the president refusing to defend him, Watt submitted a letter of resignation, suggesting that Reagan would be better served by someone else. William Clark, an old friend of the president's from California who was serving (unhappily) as National Security Adviser, agreed to take over the Interior Department.

Watt, however, was not alone in trying to undermine federal regulation of the environment. President Reagan selected Anne Gorsuch Burford, an ally of Watt's to head the Environmental Protection Administration. She, in turn, appointed Edwin Meese protégée Rita Lavelle to oversee the "Superfund" program Congress created to clean up the nation's worst hazardous waste sites. Both administrators acted in ways that subverted the very purpose of the agency they worked for.

Burford and Lavelle insisted that EPA rules unfairly restricted the chemical industry and put too great a priority on preserving a pristine environment. Environmentalists charged that the EPA adopted policies that favored polluters and also mismanaged funds. Congressional committees reported that Burford had, indeed, manipulated the Superfund for political gain by selectively distributing clean-up money. Burford resigned from the EPA and Lavelle lost her job after someone leaked a memo she wrote accusing the agency's career staff of "systematically alienating the business community." Subsequently, she was convicted of lying to Congress and sentenced to prison.

By 1984, some two dozen top EPA appointees had been removed from office or resigned under pressure. Most of their offenses involved favoritism toward the industries they were supposed to oversee. The House Energy and Commerce Oversight Subcommittee concluded in a report issued that August that over the past three years top-level officials of the EPA "violated their public trust by disregarding the public health and the environment, manipulating the Superfund program for political purposes, engaging in unethical conduct, and participating in other abuses."

Agencies headed by other Reagan appointees engaged in similar efforts to undermine safety standards. For example, the National Highway Traffic Safety Administration decided to save automobile manufacturers money by permitting new cars to carry less substantial (and less safe) bumpers. The Department of Energy and the Nuclear Regulatory Commission ignored mounting evidence of problems in the nuclear industry. Civilian power plants were seldom penalized for safety violations.

Several thousand military facilities, especially those producing nuclear weapons, suffered such grave on-site pollution that many had to be shut down completely by the end of the decade. In a misguided effort to save relatively small amounts of money while accelerating production, the Reagan administration scrimped on maintenance and safety needs. The origin of these problems predated the Reagan years. Indeed, many could be traced back to the crash program to build the first atomic bombs. But in the 1980s, as in years past, officials feared the embarrassment of disclosure and that public scrutiny would divert money from military projects.

Lewis D. Walker, named in 1980 as Deputy Assistant Secretary of the Army for environment, safety, and occupation health, admitted that the "Army considered what was inside the fences [of the nuclear facilities] our problem, and no one should know about that." But as chemical and radioactive pollution seeped outside the fences, communities and local officials began to raise objections to the web of secrecy.

The full dimensions of the problem only began to appear in 1989 when Congress pressed the Defense and Energy departments to report on environmental dangers at thousands of military facilities around the country. Preliminary surveys suggest that a cleanup may take thirty years and cost between $200 and $400 billion dollars.

By 1984, one congressional estimate counted fifty cases of misconduct, mismanagement, or fraud by high administration officials. The biggest scandals of the Reagan era, however, such as those involving the Department of Housing and Urban Development, defense contractors, and the Savings and Loan industry, stemmed mostly from corruption made inevitable by ideological fervor.

Wedtech

In 1984, while speaking at New York City's Waldorf Astoria Hotel, President Reagan turned to a familiar theme: the virtues of hard work, honesty, and spunk. The spotlight turned from the president to a member of the audience. "John Mariotta," Reagan declared, is providing jobs and training for the hard-core unemployed of the South Bronx." This businessman's "faith in God," had "moved mountains, helping hundreds of people who had almost given up hope." People like Mariotta, the president asserted, "are heroes for the eighties."

John Mariotta, the son of poor Puerto Rican immigrants, first came to Reagan's attention in 1982, during a White House meeting on urban enterprise zones, a favorite idea the president had for encouraging business in poor neighborhoods through special tax breaks. Mariotta headed the Welbilt Electronic Die Corporation (renamed Wedtech in 1983), a machine shop in the impoverished South Bronx that had become a small-scale military contractor. Speaking at the White House seminar, he recalled a confrontation he had with a drug dealer on the street near his business. "Bug out, John," the pusher yelled. "What I'm doing with our people is nothing worse than what this society is doing with our people. It's killing our people by giving them opium—the opium of welfare!" Turning to his host, Mariotta said: "Mr. President, you're killing the taxpayer of this country by strapping welfare on the backs of the taxpayer. Let me explain to you what Welbilt is doing."

As Reagan listened intently, Mariotta declared that by employing a thousand former welfare recipients, he saved the government $25 million and generated $100 million in new business. Ten similar companies in the Bronx would create over $1 billion. "Spread this penicillin to a hundred cities and you will save one hundred billion dollars." As the meeting ended, Reagan remarked that "if we had more people who could motivate like yourself, we could put a handle on this situation." Clearly, one evangelist had found another.

By 1985 Wedtech had grown into a mid-sized defense contractor with well over a thousand employees in several states and handled hundreds of millions of dollars worth of orders from the Army and Navy. By then a publicly traded corporation, its top executives became millionaires. The collapse of the firm came even more suddenly. In December 1986 Wedtech declared bankruptcy and its executives, consultants, and "friends" in Washington faced criminal charges.

Wedtech's saga began when Mariotta, a gifted tinkerer, set up a machine shop with Fred Neuberger, a Romanian Holocaust survivor. Between 1970 and 1975, the two men operated their small sheet metal business amidst the urban decay of the South Bronx. Largely by chance, the company secured a small contract in 1975 to build filters for army helicopters.

Neuberger discovered that the Pentagon had a small set-aside program that reserved contracts for minority-owned businesses. These set asides began under President Johnson and continued under Nixon, who saw them as a way of creating a class of Republican "black capitalists." In addition to African-Americans, Hispanics and other minorities could qualify.

To get placed on the list of eligible contractors, a company had to be more than half minority owned. Wedtech did not qualify since Neuberger owned a 50% share. To get around this detail, Wedtech's two partners falsely reported that Mariotta owned a two-thirds share. Critics of minority set asides had long complained that the program invited exactly this type of fraud. Wedtech secured a small contract from the Air Force in 1976 to build a jet engine part. Soon, New York Congressman Mario Biaggi, who represented a nearby district, convinced the Wedtech management to hire his private law firm as a "consultant" for $20,000 annually. Without identifying himself as a paid Wedtech lobbyist, Biaggi pressed federal agencies to grant the company additional contracts. This influence peddling worked, as more defense orders came Wedtech's way.

When the company needed fresh capital to expand operations, it found a new friend in Congressman Robert Garcia. In return for substantial payments funneled through his sister's church,[1] Garcia convinced the Small Business Administration to make generous loans to Wedtech.

Despite this promising start, Wedtech had difficulty securing a large contract it sought from the Army to build engines. Wedtech's $40 million bid to fill the order was rejected by Army procurement officers who considered the cost excessive and the company not competent to do the job. In 1981, Mariotta and Neuberger surmounted this hurdle. They hired E. Robert Wallach, a lawyer and close friend of White House counsel Edwin Meese, as a consultant.

Wallach, who eventually earned over $1 million from the company, sensed that Wedtech would appeal to the Reagan administration as a sort of "poster child." After all, its co-founder was a conservative, evangelical Christian who railed against welfare and sought to build a major industry in a ghetto. Wallach bombarded Meese with requests that he press the Defense Department to award the disputed contract to Wedtech. Meese passed on the request to his subordinates who leaned on the Defense Department. Shortly thereafter, Wedtech secured the engine contract.

Emboldened by success, Mariotta and Neuberger hired several additional consultants on friendly terms with administration officials and members of Congress. The company made large monetary contributions to the political campaigns of New York area politicians. Meanwhile, Wedtech executives siphoned off substantial amounts of company cash through illegal transactions. The president's aides, as Wallach guessed, saw the company's growth as an ideological marketing tool. They invited John Mariotta to the previously mentioned White House conference where Reagan congratulated Wedtech's founder. This became the political equivalent of a laying on of hands. A short time later, when White House aide Lyn Nofziger left the administration to open a lobbying firm, he took on Wedtech as a high paying client and began pressing

---

[1] In a twist almost too bizarre to imagine, Congressman Garcia's sister, a church minister, had helped deliver the "hush money" that Reverend Jim Bakker had paid to Jessica Hahn in the aforementioned PTL scandal.

federal agencies to give it additional contracts. As new business came his way, Mariotta declared that Wedtech's success came through a "joint venture between our silent partner, God, and the Ronald Reagans of our society."

Between 1982 and 1985, Wedtech seemed like a textbook success story. It received additional federal and private loans to expand production facilities, secured more defense contracts for engines and navy pontoons, and transformed itself into a publicly traded stock corporation. The original owners and new managers became millionaires by selling their substantial shares of stock. However, in the act of becoming a publicly owned corporation, Wedtech lost its already questionable status as a minority-owned business eligible for set asides. Since minority status had given it privileged access to government loans and contracts, the company faced a crisis. To save the day and secure a lucrative navy contract it had bid on, Wedtech officers simply bribed a federal official who recertified it as a qualified minority firm.

Even while President Reagan publicly praised Mariotta as a "hero," Wedtech perched on the edge of collapse. By 1984, its massive payoffs to consultants as well as various city, state, and federal officials drained cash reserves. Nor could the company produce most of the engines or pontoons for which it had already received substantial payment. To make matters worse, several rival minority-owned businesses complained that Wedtech had been improperly retained in the minority set-aside program.

E. Robert Wallach tried to rescue the company by bringing several new investors to it. They included Frank Chinn and Rusty Kent London, businessmen with shady pasts. In return for secret payments to themselves, Chinn and London funneled their clients' money into Wedtech. Wallach even convinced his friend, Attorney General Edwin Meese, to place his own investments into a trust fund managed by Chinn.

In May 1986, Wedtech again teetered on the brink of insolvency. Although the company had failed to deliver promised pontoons, the navy inexplicably renewed its pontoon order and provided vital cash advances. Abetted by corrupt accountants, the company declared itself in robust shape and sold an additional $75 million in bonds to the public.

By then, the U.S. attorney in New York, the Labor Department, Pentagon auditors, and several other law enforcement agencies had begun uncovering evidence of Wedtech's lawbreaking. By the fall of 1986, after looting what remained in the company accounts, Wedtech executives filed for bankruptcy.

In complex legal proceedings, most of the company management pled guilty to fraud. Wallach, Nofziger, Biaggi, Garcia, Chinn, and several military procurement officers and officials of the Small Business Administration were convicted of involvement in the scheme. Nofziger had his conviction overturned on appeal, in part because of the arcane nature of the 1978 Ethics in Government Act. Attorney General Meese, who escaped indictment, admitted putting in a word for Wedtech and helping Wallach pursue other dubious business ventures such as an oil pipeline in the Middle East. Several of his top aides quit the Justice Department in disgust. The company's failure resulted in a several hundred million dollar loss to the government and left private investors holding millions of dollars worth of valueless stocks and bonds.

The Biggest Bank Job Ever

Before 1982, the common view of the 3,200 individual Savings and Loans (S&Ls), or "thrift institutions" as they were known in the banking trade, resembled that presented in the 1946 Frank Capra film *It's A Wonderful Life*. Jimmy Stewart, a Hollywood friend of Ronald Reagan's, portrayed a small-town hero George Bailey whose thrift loaned money for the purchase of single-family homes. Although the film celebrated the neighborliness of the home loan business, in an ironic twist the goodhearted Stewart character got into serious trouble by making unwise loans to friends.

For decades, the joke ran, the thrift industry operated according to the "3–6–3" rule: pay 3% interest on deposits; loan out money at 6%; close up at 3 P.M. and head for the golf course. Because most home mortgages were small and the properties well secured, S&Ls represented a stable, useful, and low-profit segment of the nation's credit system. Since 1934, depositors' accounts were insured by the Federal Savings and Loan Insurance Corporation

(FSLIC), a New Deal innovation to restore confidence in the banking system.

For nearly forty years the system worked well. As long as inflation remained low, it did not matter that S&L assets were tied up in fixed-rate thirty-year home mortgages. But during the 1970s thrifts lost a large number of depositors because they paid out only 5.5% interest on deposits. When inflation reached 13% in 1979, unregulated money market funds paid double the interest rate offered by the S&Ls. Naturally, savers moved their funds to the uninsured but high-yield money funds.

In 1972, S&Ls had a collective net worth of almost $17 billion. By 1980, they had a *negative* worth of at least that amount. At least eight out of ten thrifts were losing money. These massive losses prevented S&Ls from making mortgage loans for home buyers and this, in turn, hurt the entire economy.

To make thrifts and banks (which suffered similar, if less severe, problems) more competitive, and stimulate the housing industry, Congress, which received generous campaign contributions from S&L lobbyists, agreed in 1980 to boost federal deposit insurance from $40,000 up to $100,000 per account (an individual could have several accounts) and to allow payment of higher interest rates. These decisions were quite popular and Congress acted without extensive debate or hearings.

The 1980 reforms helped S&Ls attract new deposits, but failed to resolve the fact that thrift institutions continued to earn low rates of return on home mortgages. To keep S&Ls afloat, a way had to be found for them to earn higher rates of return on investments so they could pay the higher interest rates they were now permitted to offer. In 1982, the Reagan administration and key members of Congress concluded that the solution to this problem would come through the comprehensive de-regulation of the Savings and Loan industry.

On October 15, 1982, Ronald Reagan appeared before photographers to sign a major piece of legislation, the Garn-St. Germain Act, de-regulating the thrift industry. Named after Democratic House Banking Chairman Fernand St. Germain of Rhode Island and Utah Republican Senator Jake Garn, the new law, in Reagan's words, represented the "most important legislation for financial institutions in fifty years." It would assure more housing, jobs, and growth. "All in all," the president crowed, "I think we've hit the jackpot."

The lobbying organization representing S&Ls agreed. Its spokesman called Garn-St. Germain the "Emancipation Proclamation for America's savings institutions." At the end of the signing ceremony, the president passed around the several pens he had used to afix his signature. In fact, Reagan had just written, as one financial expert observed a decade later, "the largest check in history, drawn on the collective bank account of the American taxpayer." Within six years the S&L industry teetered on the brink of a chasm. Hundreds of thrifts had failed, and taxpayers faced mounting obligations that might total a staggering $500 billion over the next forty years.

Before de-regulation, the bulk of S&L activity involved making low-risk, low-profit mortgage loans for single-family homes in the communities where the thrifts were located. After 1982 they were free to operate their own money market funds and to invest about 40% of their assets in raw land, commercial real estate, shopping malls, art work, junk bonds, bull-sperm banks, and virtually anything else. The new law eased rules for buying or starting up a savings and loan, relaxed accounting standards, and permitted owners to invest little of their own cash in the venture. Some of the later problems might have been mitigated by careful scrutiny of S&L operations. But even as the thrift industry grew, the Reagan administration cut the number of examiners charged with supervising its books.

Without question, the new investment portfolios promised a greater possible return than mortgages on single-family homes. They also carried far more risk. The risk, however, was not born directly by those owning an S&L. Federal deposit insurance meant that neither the thrift owners—who invested depositors' money— nor the depositors themselves (up to $100,000 per account) risked losing anything. On the other hand, thrift owners could keep most of the profits from speculative ventures that paid off.

President Reagan predicted these measures would liberate the creative energy of lenders and produce profits that would ultimately make more money available for home loans. Practice defied this neat theory. Speculators, looking for a base of operations, bought up many small, locally owned S&Ls. To attract large amounts of cash quickly they solicited from money brokers so-called jumbo $100,000 deposits that paid especially high interest. These brokered accounts, rather than local deposits, formed the bulk of the new money coming into S&L coffers.

Those able to make jumbo deposits had the best of both worlds—high yield and complete safety. Of course, to afford the top rates paid on jumbos, S&L managers had to invest in higher-yield, higher-risk projects. In many parts of the country, incompetent or corrupt thrift owners went wild investing insured funds in commercial real estate and other risky ventures.

Arizona businessman Charles Keating, for example, purchased for a few million dollars the small California-based Lincoln Federal Savings and Loan. He quickly transformed it into a multi-billion institution by paying high interest rates to attract jumbo accounts that then were invested in extremely speculative projects. Keating found other ways to use the thrift to generate money. Lincoln's tellers sold $250 million in "junk bonds" issued by American Continental (Lincoln's corporate parent) to 23,000 mostly elderly investors as part of their Individual Retirement Accounts (IRA). Tellers falsely assured gullible buyers that the junk bonds were guaranteed like regular deposits. Keating, who behaved like a sinister caricature of mythical banker George Bailey, primed his sales staff with the advice that "the weak, meek, and ignorant are always good targets."

Keating was only one of many shady operators who turned ownership of an S&L into a governmental license to print money. Yet for about five years all that most people noticed was that the spigot of easy commercial mortgage money created a construction boom in parts of the country. In practice, the FSLIC underwrote the freewheeling S&Ls that pumped billions of dollars into the economy. For all Reagan's criticism of New Deal efforts to underwrite growth, this represented a kind of federal deficit spending with an abandon that would have made Franklin Roosevelt blush.

Corrupt lenders found it simple to conspire with builders to drive up the cost of projects, leading to bigger fees for all. High costs insured that few of the ventures would ever turn a profit. Federal tax law, at least until 1986, mitigated this problem by allowing losses on real estate investments to offset income from other sources.[1]

With little danger of exposure, S&L officers found creative ways to make money at the expense of their institutions. Some made dubious loans to business partners or paid themselves exorbitant salaries. For example, in addition to paying himself a multimillion dollar salary, Charles Keating placed his children, his in-laws, and family friends on the Lincoln Savings payroll. At one point Keating took his entourage on a corporate-funded trip to Italy, telling auditors they were sampling Italian cuisine in order to evaluate the menu of a restaurant that applied for a loan. In a popular scam, properties were often "flipped" (sold back and forth) several times in a day for ever higher prices, with thrift managers authorizing escalating loans in return for kickbacks.

Although the degree of fraud remained unclear until after Reagan left office, problems in the de-regulated industry surfaced as early as 1984. Timely intervention by federal regulators might have limited the cost of the debacle. The collapse of the Penn Square (Oklahoma) bank and bailout of Continental Illinois Bank in 1983–84 sounded warning signals. But Reagan's budget cuts had reduced the power and number of bank examiners. Also, the president had appointed his former assistant press secretary from Sacramento, Ed

[1] The tax reform act promoted by Reagan and passed by Congress in 1986 altered the rules in ways that affected S&Ls adversely. Investors could no longer write off passive losses they incurred from real estate by deducting it from other sources of income. For example, an affluent physician might invest in a partnership that bought an office building in Houston. The rents received from tenants often did not cover the cost of mortgage payments the partnership had to pay the S&L that gave them the loan to purchase the building. Until 1986, a portion of the operating loss could be deducted from the physician's other sources of income. The members of the partnership could also reap a profit if the building appreciated in value and they later sold it. The new tax law limited the deductibility of real estate investment losses. Unable to offset the loss, owners frequently defaulted on the loan. The S&L then repossessed the building. As was often the case due to bad judgment or fraud, the property had been overvalued. When an S&L could not resell the property for enough money to cover the outstanding loan, it absorbed a loss. Replayed many times, this scenario forced thrift institutions into insolvency.

Gray, to head the Federal Home Loan Bank Board (FHLBB) which monitored S&Ls.

By his own account, when Gray accepted the post he had little familiarity with the industry but believed fully in Reagan's ideas of de-regulation. "I was appointed because it was thought that I would be a patsy for the industry," Gray later reported. Gray began his stewardship by fulfilling the industry's hopes. Gradually, however, he realized the scope of the impending disaster and tried to stem the excesses. In 1984, several thrift institutions collapsed, at a cost of a few hundred million dollars. Gray called for limiting use of the large brokered accounts, tightening lending rules, and hiring more bank examiners. Treasury Secretary Donald Regan (whose old employer, Merrill, Lynch did a thriving business in placing brokered accounts) as well as the Democratic Speaker of the House, Texas Congressman Jim Wright (whose close friend and business partner owned an S&L) thwarted the move. In 1985, White House insiders denounced Gray as a "re-regulator" and urged him to resign.

Auditors uncovered severe problems with Lincoln Savings as early as 1985. It held only $54 million in passbook accounts, over $2 billion in jumbo accounts placed by money brokers, and paid Charles Keating and his many relatives huge salaries. To meet the interest on the jumbo accounts, Lincoln had invested in especially risky commercial real estate. When Gray urged that Keating and other speculators be forced to place more of their own money, and less of depositors' federally insured money, at risk, Keating counter-attacked. He urged friends in the Reagan administration to dismiss Gray and, when that failed, offered him a job with Lincoln Savings to get him off the Federal bank board.

By 1986 the insurance reserve fund of the FSLIC had fallen to $2.5 billion, down from $6 billion in 1984. Since it cost up to $500 million to close down and assume the liabilities of a single mid-sized thrift and dozens of thrifts faced default, Ed Gray urged Congress to appropriate an additional $15 to 25 billion for the FSLIC. Much of the money would come from higher insurance premiums charged to S&Ls. The honest thrifts objected to paying for the sins of others; the dishonest thrifts could not afford to pay;

and both the Reagan administration and House Speaker Jim Wright charged that the higher insurance levy would ruin the industry.

Congress eventually appropriated $10 billion to bolster the insurance fund. But instead of tightening supervision, the president nominated Lee Henkel, an associate of Charles Keating, to an open seat on the Federal Home Loan Bank Board. He withdrew only when reports surfaced that linked him to questionable business activities. Still, Keating had other arrows in his quiver.

During the previous few years Keating contributed about $3 million to political candidates, about half of it to five senators, including Alan Cranston of California, John McCain and Dennis DeConcini of Arizona, Don Riegle of Michigan, and John Glenn of Ohio. He also provided jobs to former members of their staffs and made loans to them on favorable terms. Lincoln, and parent company American Continental Corporation, had operations in all their states. In April 1987, the five senators called Gray to a meeting in which they asked him to exempt Lincoln Savings from rules requiring it to put more of its own cash into its reserves. Gray refused and noted that bank examiners would probably recommend closure of Lincoln.

The next month Gray's term on the FHLBB ended. In June President Reagan replaced him as chairman with M. Danny Wall, an aide to Senator Jake Garn of Utah, the co-author of the deregulation act. Wall quickly interceded on behalf of Lincoln Savings by overruling the bank examiners and allowing the thrift to remain in operation while an audit continued. Nearly two years passed before examiners received permission to close Lincoln. By then (April 1989) the FSLIC had to assume liabilities of some $2.5 billion.

While difficult to prove, congressional testimony and other evidence suggests that Wall purposely downplayed the dimensions of the Savings and Loan crisis for two critical years (June 1987 through early 1989) as a favor to President Reagan and Republican presidential candidate George Bush. His repeated assurances, despite hard facts to the contrary, that the industry faced only minor problems, eliminated a major political problem for Reagan and his likely successor. Bipartisan collaboration, of course, made the cover up work. Enough Democratic senators and representatives had received campaign funds from the S&L industry that they had little incentive to arouse voters' wrath. As late as 1986, economists believe, the cost of an S&L bailout might have been contained at "only" $100 billion.

The public remained relatively undisturbed by the dimensions of this crisis. For one thing, no citizen lost a dime in a savings account. The FSLIC, one of the New Deal agencies so unpalatable to Ronald Reagan, guaranteed all deposits and prevented panic. But the losses were so large that taxpayers would have to bear most of the cost of the bailout. Perhaps the very size of the S&L crisis made it difficult to understand. Americans had a vivid image of bank robberies, even though they involved relatively petty sums of cash. For example, in 1985 6,000 bank robberies netted gunmen about $50 million. The cost of assuming the liabilities of Lincoln Savings alone in 1989 totaled about *fifty times as much* money. Apprehending and convicting armed robbers, however, proved simple in comparison to explaining the investment scams perpetrated by someone like Charles Keating. The fact that an S&L owner committed robbery with a pen rather than a gun muddied the water. A California court convicted Keating of fraud in December 1991. That same month the federal government indicted him. Although numerous S&L operators were charged with crimes, most of the money had disappeared.

By 1991, over 600 S&Ls had failed and less than half of the remaining 2,500 stood much chance of surviving. The federal government created the Resolution Trust Corporation to take over a huge inventory of vacant buildings and obligations from the failed thrifts. Some economists estimate the bailout may eventually cost $500 billion spread over several decades. By any measure, this was the biggest bank heist in the nation's history.

The HUD Scandal

Along with the Department of Education, no federal agency grated more uncomfortably on Reagan than the Department of Housing and Urban Development (HUD). A legacy of the Great Society programs of the 1960s, it promoted housing construction for people of limited means using tax dollars paid to developers. It struck

Secretary of Housing and Urban Development Samuel Pierce defends his performance before Congress. *Courtesy AP/Wide World Photos.*

conservatives as a prime example of government encroachment on the private sector.

The Reagan administration's attitude toward the Department of Housing and Urban Development seemed captured by the president's relationship to the man he appointed to head the department. Samuel Pierce ("Silent Sam," as aides called him) was a Wall Street lawyer, Republican, and African-American. He had little familiarity with public housing programs and seemed selected for the post largely because Reagan wanted a pliant minority representative in his Cabinet. Pierce was the only member of the Cabinet to serve eight years, yet he had so little contact with Reagan that at a reception for mayors the President walked up to him and said "How do you do, Mr. Mayor?"

Reagan and Budget Director David Stockman slashed HUD's budget, personnel, and programs. Between 1981 and 1987, the agencies budget fell from over $33 billion per year to $14 billion. Career officials lost their jobs, transferred to other agencies, or became disillusioned time servers. As experienced civil servants departed, the White House replaced many with political appointees who either knew nothing about housing or actively opposed the agency's program. Typical among them was Emmanuel S. Savas, an assistant secretary who spent much of his time at HUD writing a book (which his employees had to type and proofread) entitled

Privatizing the Public Sector: How to Shrink Government. Savas resigned when his activities came to light, but others like him stayed on.

HUD stood out as a cash cow ripe for plunder. Some agency officials steered contracts to influential Republicans hired as consultants by housing developers. Pierce delegated much of his authority to Debora Gore Dean, a young assistant who later told interviewers that she considered that the housing program was "set up and designed to be a political program."

Several officials who had previously worked for HUD or had ties to the White House began lucrative careers consulting with construction companies seeking federal funds. For example, former Interior Secretary James G. Watt earned nearly a half million dollars after he left government merely by placing a few phone calls to friends in HUD on behalf of a company that sought backing for three housing projects. When asked by congressional investigators to justify his fee, Watt declared that while the "system was flawed," there was no reason why he should not profit from it.

Investigators surmise that Pierce and his deputies allowed several billion dollars from HUD coffers to be used partly as a private fund to award contracts to friends and political cronies. Soon after Reagan left office, investigators discovered that large amounts of money had been spent to subsidize the construction of luxury apartments, golf courses, swimming pools, and on outright scams, rather than on building low-income housing. Friends and relatives of New York Senator Alfonse D'Amato fared especially well in getting HUD to subsidize pet projects.

In a 1990 report on the scandal, the House Government Operations Committee concluded that throughout the Reagan years HUD was "enveloped by influence peddling, favoritism abuse, greed, fraud, embezzlement and theft." Several low-level HUD employees were convicted of crimes. Samuel Pierce refused to testify before Congress and (as of 1991) remains under the scrutiny of a special prosecutor weighing a criminal indictment.

Conclusion

Neither during his presidency nor in his post-presidential statements did Ronald Reagan ever discuss the Savings and Loan crisis or the Wedtech or HUD scandals. While he spoke with pride about the "regulatory relief" his administration brought to the American people, he dissociated himself completely from the scandals that permeated EPA, HUD, and the thrift industry. Reagan had a knack of making bad news disappear simply by ignoring it. The American people, polls revealed, seldom associated him personally with any of the scandals or failures of his administration. Reagan's invulnerability to negative events represented "Teflon" with a vengeance.

5

Tall in the Saddle:
Reagan and the New Cold War

A FEW DAYS before his first summit meeting with Soviet leader Mikhail Gorbachev in 1985, Ronald Reagan conferred with a group of "Star War" enthusiasts that included Dr. Edward Teller, Lt. General David O. Graham, and Gregory Fossedal, an editorial writer for the *Wall Street Journal*. They urged the president to maintain his commitment to the so-called space shield and resist any temptation to use it as a bargaining chip in improving relations with Moscow. Fossedal even brought what he called a "special model" of Gorbachev for Reagan to study. As he handed over a Darth Vader doll, complete with light saber, the journalist remarked "this is the man you'll be up against." "You know," said Reagan, "they really are an evil empire."

For nearly six years, the president's antipathy toward the Soviet Union defined his foreign policy. A year before receiving the Gorbachev voodoo doll, in August 1984, he had spoken into a microphone to test sound levels before delivering a Saturday morning radio commentary. A technician had activated the circuit prematurely, resulting in the broadcast of some unscripted remarks. "My fellow Americans," Reagan declared, "I'm pleased to tell you today that I've signed legislation that will outlaw the Soviet Union forever. We begin bombing in five minutes." Although the president laughed off the reaction to what he said, the men in the Kremlin considered it a real threat. They instructed KGB intelligence officers in Washington to report signs of war preparation such as stockpiling food or blood in federal buildings.

During his first term in the White House, Reagan described the Soviet Union as the "focus of evil in the modern world" led by men who reserved the right to "lie, cheat and steal" their way to world domination. He went so far as to insist that a Soviet conspiracy "underlies all the unrest that is going on. If they weren't engaged in this game of dominoes, there wouldn't be any hot spots in the world."

Yet, in his final year as president, Reagan presided over a dramatic improvement in Soviet-American relations. By the time he left office, the president and his counterpart in the Kremlin had toasted each other as "Ronnie and Mikhail" and signed a treaty destroying a whole category of nuclear missiles. Opinion polls reported Americans feeling friendlier toward the Soviet Union than at any time since the end of World War II. The public that elected Reagan as a cold warrior applauded him as a peacemaker. When Reagan retired, 72% of Americans voiced strong approval for his handling of foreign policy.

Oil shocks, inflation, terrorist attacks, renewed fears of Soviet expansion, and, above all, the Iranian hostage crisis in the late 1970s had created an impression of national weakness that Ronald Reagan exploited in the election of 1980. He insisted "there *are* simple answers" to complex questions. Reagan complained that America suffered from a "Vietnam syndrome," the inability or unwillingness to resist Soviet pressure and defend American friends and interests abroad. Attributing this weakness to guilt feelings over the Vietnam War, Reagan praised that struggle as a noble cause. His first Secretary of State, Gen. Alexander Haig, echoed this sentiment, declaring the time had come to "shed the sackcloth and ashes" worn by Americans for a decade. Reagan pledged to restore military superiority, defend foreign allies, and support anti-communist movements throughout the world.

A 1979 article by Jeane Kirkpatrick that appeared in *Commentary* magazine influenced Reagan's views greatly. Jimmy Carter's "lack of realism," Kirkpatrick wrote, not "deep historical forces," drove old friends like the Shah of Iran and Nicaragua's Anastasio Somoza from power. Carter's failure to support these strongmen

The President and U.N. Ambassador Jeane Kirkpatrick. *Courtesy U.S. National Archives.*

hastened the triumph of regimes hostile to the United States. It made more sense for the United States to support "positively friendly" autocrats and "right wing autocracies" since, unlike totalitarian regimes of the left, they "do sometimes evolve into democracies."

This analysis confirmed Reagan's sentiments. For example, he described a conversation with a former aide to the Shah of Iran who told him that if the old regime had been permitted to "arrest five hundred people," they could have "headed off the revolution." Instead, he took the advice of the American Embassy "to do nothing" and the Islamic fundamentalists took power. It was as simple as that. After he won the election, Reagan named Kirkpatrick the Ambassador to the United Nations.

Americans generally liked the new President's tough but inspirational inaugural message to "dream heroic dreams." Reducing complex international questions to a list of rights and wrongs, he predicted that spiritual renewal and rearmament would quash terrorism and reduce the risk of a Soviet attack. His appearance of resolve seemed enhanced by the fact that just as he completed his inaugural remarks on January 20, 1981, Iran released the fifty-two Americans held in captivity for 444 days. Even though Carter had negotiated the terms of the settlement, Reagan implied that the Ayatollah knew better than to tussle with the "Gipper."

Reagan's Foreign Policy Style

As with the president's domestic program, a yawning gap existed between the rhetoric and reality of foreign policy. Ronald Reagan lived in a world of myths and symbols, rather than facts and programs. In spite of his reputation as an ideological activist, the president gave little specific direction to his foreign policy advisers. Until 1983, it is uncertain whether Reagan even thought in terms of a coherent strategy. He and his advisers were determined to stress domestic issues during the first two years of office. Foreign policy consisted largely of assertive rhetoric, the arms buildup, and covert paramilitary operations. Reagan hoped these actions would wring concessions from Moscow and reduce Soviet influence.

The president often began National Security Council meetings by reading letters or press clippings sent to him by citizens. Each week the White House Communications Office (called by some irreverent staff members the "Schlock Capital of the World" because of the many needlepoint inspirational sayings and similar items sent by the president's admirers) selected about thirty letters for Reagan to read. On Friday afternoons he answered many of these in longhand notes. He devoted more time to this than to scheduled meetings with many of his senior Cabinet members.

When the president was under the influence of these letters, Chief of Staff Donald Regan later remarked, the "goddamnest things would come out of him. We had to watch what he read." But after he read a few letters or told an anecdote, the president usually fell silent and seldom asked questions. After a few minutes, he soon exhibited what aides called a "glassy look."

In 1981 Reagan named former Henry Kissinger aide and Nixon chief of staff Gen. Alexander Haig as Secretary of State. The president promised him full authority to act as "Vicar of Foreign Policy," in Haig's phrase and the new Secretary of State lost no time in trying to assert his leadership. On inauguration day he handed Edwin Meese a memorandum on his priorities and awaited the president's reply. When none came, he asked Meese what had happened. Meese told him it "was lost," which should have, but did not, shatter Haig's illusions.

During the first months of the new administration, Haig urged Reagan to confront the guerrillas in El Salvador and Fidel Castro's Cuba. "Give me the word and I'll make that island a fucking parking lot," Michael Deaver recorded him as shouting. According to Deaver, Haig's fury "scared the shit" out of Reagan and prompted the White House staff to undermine the Secretary of State at every turn.

Haig lasted 18 unhappy months in the State Department before Reagan replaced him in June 1982. Afterward, Haig described the administration's policy-making apparatus as a "ghost ship." You heard "the creak of the rigging and the groan of the timbers and sometimes even glimpsed the crew on deck . . . but which of the crew had the helm . . . was impossible to know for sure."

Throughout the first term, the White House triumvirate of James Baker, Michael Deaver, and Edwin Meese influenced foreign policy by controlling access to Reagan. For example, Haig seldom got into the Oval Office, never alone. The White House guard knew that failure to monitor Reagan's visitors sometimes led to radical changes in policy. For example, in 1983 Joseph Coors, a friend of the president's, escorted nuclear physicist Edward Teller past the presidential doorkeeper. Teller beguiled the president with exaggerated stories of an anti-missile defense. Shortly afterward, "Star Wars" emerged as a national priority.

Except on a few points, Reagan preferred to follow the lead of his advisers on foreign policy matters. This presented a problem since many disagreed among themselves. In the absence of any direction besides anti-communism, Secretary of State Haig (replaced by George Shultz in 1982), Secretary of Defense Caspar Weinberger, CIA director William Casey, and six successive directors of the National Security Council (Richard Allen, William Clark, Robert McFarlane, John Poindexter, Frank Carlucci, and Colin Powell) often followed their own instincts. For example, Secretary of State Shultz supported negotiations with the Soviets over arms control and a punitive military approach toward minor enemies, such as the Sandinistas in Nicaragua. Secretary of Defense Caspar Weinberger distrusted the Soviets completely and favored an arms buildup over any agreement to limit armaments.

Yet Weinberger proved quite reluctant to use military force in the Third World, lest it undermine public support for rearmament. At one cabinet meeting an exasperated Shultz snapped, "If you are not willing to use force, maybe we should cut your budget." Reagan tried to settle disputes among his contentious advisers by asking them to compromise, a solution NSC head Robert McFarlane described as "intrinsically unworkable."

Enhanced CIA power to conduct paramilitary operations in the Third World emerged as one of the two pillars (the other being rearmament) of Reagan foreign policy through 1987. The president appointed William Casey, his friend and campaign manager, to head the intelligence agency. Casey had served in the Office of Strategic Services during World War II and had earned a fortune on Wall Street. He made the CIA a key player in the battle against Soviet influence in the Third World.

The president's three chief White House aides during the first term, Baker, Deaver, and Meese, worried about the influence exercised over their boss by the CIA director. Casey, Deaver recalled "played to Reagan's dark side." The spy chief's habit of mumbling words and the president's impaired hearing and failure to ask questions often left staff unsure what the two men had discussed or agreed to. After private Reagan-Casey meetings, Michael Deaver would ask the president what the two of them had discussed. If the CIA director had sold Reagan on some particularly wild scheme, Deaver informed James Baker who sent along some trusted intermediary (often the First Lady) to talk the president out of it.

Reagan backed Casey's effort to rebuild CIA paramilitary strength and convinced Congress to abandon Carter-era restraints on many covert operations. Over the next few years the CIA funded anticommunist guerrillas active in Angola, Mozambique, Afghanistan, and Central America. The administration believed that "low intensity warfare," a term for counterinsurgency operations, was a relatively cheap and fairly safe way to battle Moscow for global influence. Covert warfare minimized the risk of confronting the Soviets while allowing the administration freedom to act with minimal congressional oversight.

In another break with his predecessor, Reagan endorsed ambassador Jeane Kirkpatrick's confrontational style at the UN. She frequently criticized UN agencies and many Third World states for not supporting American actions without question. To show his dislike for the world body, the president withheld financial support and suspended American participation in one of its main subsidiaries, the United Nations Economic, Scientific, and Cultural Organization (UNESCO).

The administration followed Kirkpatrick's idea of supporting friendly autocrats to justify Reagan's reluctance to impose sanctions on the racist South African regime or to criticize human rights abuses perpetrated by pro-American governments in El Salvador, Guatemala, Chile, Haiti, the Philippines, and Pakistan. The president supported dictators such as Ferdinand Marcos of the Philippines and Haiti's Jean-Claude (Baby Doc) Duvalier even as popular insurrections undermined their power. Only after it became clear that they might be toppled by leftist forces did Reagan agree to withdraw favor from these strongmen.

Elsewhere in the Third World, the Reagan administration's misgivings about government's playing any positive role in economic development and social change affected the pattern of foreign aid. Accentuating a trend, nearly all American assistance flowed to a handful of countries, generally for military purposes. Israel and Egypt received several billion dollars annually, followed by the Philippines, Turkey, Pakistan, and El Salvador. These six nations accounted for nearly three-fourths of all foreign aid. The United States devoted less than one-third of 1% of its GNP to helping others, a lower percentage than any other industrialized democracy.

Reagan's gut anti-communism did not prevent him from muting his feelings and acting pragmatically when required. Jimmy Carter's 1978 decision to cut formal links with Taiwan and establish regular diplomatic ties with China had infuriated Reagan. He hinted that if elected president he might restore relations with Taiwan, whose government he described as "an American ally." He also promised to sell Taiwan weapons, regardless of China's opposition.

During the first two years of the Reagan administration, relations between Beijing and Washington grew so frosty that China even threatened to downgrade relations with the United States if America sold weapons to Taiwan. But both nations overcame their principles. The United States needed China's help in supporting the Afghan guerrillas fighting Soviet troops and valued Beijing's anti-Soviet stance. Chinese leaders recognized their dependence upon western technology, trade, and loans for modernization.

In August 1982 the two nations reached an accord that recognized the right of the United States to sell weapons to Taiwan so long as Washington promised to "reduce gradually its sales." Both sides represented this agreement as a victory for their position. President Reagan ceased making his anti-Chinese, pro-Taiwan statements. China's leaders invited him on a state visit early in 1984 which provided the president with attractive visual images for his upcoming re-election campaign. In China, Ronald and Nancy visited historic sites, cooed at the pandas in Beijing's zoo, shopped at a farmer's market, and avoided criticizing their hosts. Over the next four years, Reagan seldom mentioned the world's largest communist nation.

More Bang for More Bucks: The New Arms Race

More than anything, the staggering arms buildup begun in 1981 emerged as the centerpiece of Reagan's foreign policy. Defense spending rose steadily through 1985, peaking at just over $300 billion per year. At full throttle, the Pentagon spent over $30 per hour, every day on procuring weapons, maintaining forces, and exploring new technologies. The administration, many suspected, believed a stepped-up arms race would beggar the Soviet Union. To a degree, this may have proved true, though at a great cost to the United States as well.

During this period, the United States, in effect, substituted an arms budget and covert operations for foreign policy. The administration invested heavily in weapons designed during the Ford-

Reagan shows Nancy the guns of the U.S.S. *Iowa. Courtesy U.S. National Archives.*

Carter years, many of which were envisioned for fighting a nuclear war with the Soviet Union. These included enhanced radiation neutron bombs and artillery shells designed to irradiate Soviet tanks and troops in central Europe; 100 MX intercontinental missiles capable of carrying ten nuclear warheads with pinpoint accuracy into Soviet territory; the B-1 intercontinental bomber (cancelled by Carter but revived by Reagan) to replace the fleet of aging B-52s; the B-2 or "stealth" bomber and "stealth" fighter, secret radar-avoiding planes able to penetrate deep inside the Soviet Union; powerful and highly accurate D-5 missiles for mounting on Trident submarines; cruise missiles and Pershing II missiles which, when launched from Europe could hit targets inside Russia in a few minutes; and a 600-ship navy.

Mounting Anxiety over Arms

These immensely powerful and expensive weapons sparked a great deal of controversy. Critics of the MX missile complained that its power and accuracy meant that in a crisis the Soviets would be tempted to strike first in order to destroy the missiles in their vulnerable silos before they could be launched. (After Utah's two Republican senators, Jake Garn and Orin Hatch, objected to basing the MX in multiple shelters in their state as Carter had proposed, Reagan opted to put the new missile into existing but "hardened" Minuteman silos. Experts doubted these could withstand a nuclear attack.) American commanders, knowing this, might feel impelled to fire the missiles first, lest the Soviets score an early knockout. Thus, instead of enhancing deterrence, the MX might create a hair-trigger situation in which both sides struck first out of fear.

Until 1986, the Democratic-controlled House and Republican Senate approved most of Reagan's arms requests. Like the public, many Democratic representatives favored a more assertive foreign policy and appreciated the president's tough rhetoric. Also, the results of two decades of effort to negotiate arms limitations with the Soviets seemed to have borne little fruit. The Democratic Party suffered an intense identity crisis, persisting since the Iran stalemate, which diffused organized opposition to the administration's foreign and military policies.

Nevertheless, many ordinary citizens expressed anxiety over the new arms race. In 1982 journalist Jonathan Schell published *The Fate of the Earth,* a graphic, bestselling account of the effect of a single hydrogen bomb on New York City. Over the next two years the Nuclear Freeze Movement, a grass roots organization, led large demonstrations calling on both superpowers to cease building new weapons. In 1982 seventeen senators and 128 House members supported a resolution to this effect. The next year, the House of Representatives voted in favor of a freeze.

Stung by this criticism, Reagan accused some anti-nuclear groups of acting under communist influence. In fact, a large number of Roman Catholic bishops took an anti-nuclear stand. The bishops issued a 1983 pastoral letter condemning nuclear weapons as "immoral." They decried the arms race "which robs the poor and the vulnerable" and places "before humankind the indefensible choices of constant terror or surrender."

At least 100 million television viewers watched a docudrama that November called "The Day After." It portrayed the devastation of a nuclear war. Although polls showed much anxiety about the escalation of the arms race, the president retained sufficient support to give him the clout to push his weapons programs through Congress.

The administration adopted a contradictory policy toward arms limitations treaties. Reagan denigrated as "fatally flawed" Carter's still unratified SALT II treaty, charging that it locked in a Soviet advantage and left the United States vulnerable. The president deplored the treaty's limits and promised to develop more nuclear weapons to close the "window of vulnerability." But the Joint Chiefs of Staff disagreed with Reagan. They believed that SALT II, despite imperfections, restrained the Soviets from deploying even more missiles. Although Reagan refused to concede this point, in practice he adhered to most of the provisions of the SALT II treaty. In 1982 Reagan agreed to resume arms control talks with Moscow. But negotiations to reduce long-range missiles (Strategic Arms Reduction Talks, or START) and medium-range weapons (Intermediate Nuclear Forces, or INF) quickly foundered over political, technical, and military objections raised by both sides. In December 1983, when the United States began deployment of cruise and Pershing II missiles in Western Europe, Soviet negotiators walked out.

The Soviet Union claimed that its own intermediate range SS-20 missiles targeted on Europe merely matched British and French missiles as well as weapons aboard American planes and submarines around Europe. Washington disputed this assertion. Influenced by Defense Secretary Weinberger and his hardline deputy, Richard Perle, Reagan proposed a "Zero Option," involving the removal of all Soviet SS-20 missiles in return for no future U.S. deployment of cruise and Pershing missiles in Europe. As Weinberger and Perle hoped, this scuttled negotiations when the Soviets protested that the American stance locked in a U.S. advantage.

The domestic debate grew quite bizarre when another Weinberger aide, T. K. Jones, tried to calm popular alarm with assurances that most Americans would survive, or even prosper, after a nuclear war. Jones explained that in case of attack citizens need only "dig a hole, cover it with a couple of doors, and then throw three feet of dirt on top. If there are enough shovels around," Jones predicted, "everybody's going to make it." He forecast rapid economic recovery. To some, this glib assertion made it seem that the administration was preparing to fight a nuclear war in the belief it would be survivable.

Star Wars

Reagan held seemingly contradictory views about nuclear war. Perhaps because of his early religious upbringing, he often referred to nuclear conflict as the manifestation of Armageddon, a biblical prophesy of the destruction of the world. Since he maintained that the Bible foretold all events, this presumably meant he expected an unavoidable war. Still, the prospect of such a holocaust horrified him.

During a tour in 1979 of the Strategic Air Command center at Cheyenne Mountain in Colorado, he was shocked when told that if the Soviets fired even one missile, the United States could do nothing but track it and fire back. His friend Martin Anderson quoted Reagan as saying "we have spent all that money and have all that equipment, and there is nothing we can do to prevent a nuclear missile from hitting us." Reagan especially disliked the chilling acronym—MAD, or Mutual Assured Destruction—that described American strategy.

The president's idea of a solution to the nuclear threat stemmed partly, like many of his notions, from the movies. In the otherwise forgettable 1940 adventure film *Murder in the Air,* secret agent Brass Bancroft (Ronald Reagan) foiled the effort of foreign agents to steal a secret "inertia projector," a device that could stop enemy aircraft from flying. As one of the characters remarks, it would "make America invincible in war and therefore the greatest force for peace ever invented." Reagan often recalled the early 1950s film *The Day the Earth Stood Still* in which an alien from another planet stops all machines on Earth as a warning to mankind to seek peace.

During the late-1970s physicist Dr. Edward Teller and retired Air Force Lt. General Daniel Graham, who headed a group called High Frontier, impressed Reagan with talk of an anti-missile shield. During a 1983 meeting in the Oval Office, Teller told Reagan about progress in building an X-ray laser powered by a nuclear bomb.

In theory, the device could produce energy beams capable of shooting down Soviet missiles after their launch and before they deployed their multiple warheads. Mounted on orbiting platforms, they could provide a space shield, or "astrodome," over America. As Teller expected, the president liked the idea of a high technology "fix" and neglected to probe for details.

In March 1983, when Reagan unveiled his updated secret weapon, his words paraphrased those spoken in his 1940 film. The president revealed a startling vision of a peaceful future in which a "Strategic Defense Initiative" (SDI) would render nuclear weapons "impotent and obsolete." Reagan proposed a vast research and development program to develop an anti-missile system. Most critics, and many supporters, dubbed the concept "Star Wars."

Only a handful of White House insiders knew in advance of Reagan's initiative. The Joint Chiefs of Staff and the secretaries of state and defense were skeptics, while National Security Adviser Robert McFarlane favored SDI as a bargaining chip with the Soviets rather than as an actual system. However, the White House public relations staff had been consulted more closely. Michael Deaver arranged for testing the idea on focus groups and found solid support for a "space shield." Deaver admitted he and those queried had no idea how such a shield would work but that they liked "the concept."

Many people inside and outside the administration worried that SDI violated the ABM treaty, which barred the United States and Soviet Union from testing or deploying any new anti-missile systems. A majority of scientists doubted that Star Wars, which depended on many types of untested technology, would ever work. Even a shield 90% effective would allow through enough enemy warheads to obliterate this country. Some critics judged SDI little more than a fig leaf to mask substantial assistance for American companies engaged in high technology competition against Japan. For example, the Rockwell Corporation issued a promotional brochure for investors describing SDI as a vast new "Frontier for Growth, Leadership and Freedom." Other critics of the program speculated that SDI proponents did not really expect to shoot down missiles, but wanted to provoke Moscow into a bankrupting high technology contest.

The space shield described by the president and advertised on television by groups such as High Frontier never stood a chance of being built. The huge costs and daunting technical problems compelled weapons researchers to concentrate on developing systems to protect American *nuclear missile silos,* not cities or civilians, against a Soviet nuclear strike. They reasoned that SDI might knock out enough incoming warheads to permit sufficient American missiles to survive and launch a punishing retaliatory blow. This likelihood, presumably, would deter the Soviets from attacking. In effect, SDI would do little more than enhance, at great cost, the MAD strategy.

From Moscow's perspective, SDI appeared as one more threat. For example, the United States might launch a nuclear first strike that would destroy most Soviet missiles in their silos. An SDI anti-missile system might be good enough to shoot down a small Soviet retaliatory barrage. American leaders, confident of escaping destruction, might be tempted to initiate nuclear war under these conditions.

Between 1983 and 1989, the United States spent almost $17 billion on SDI research, but achieved few results. The much-touted X-ray laser failed to work and the estimated cost of even a limited space shield literally skyrocketed. The disappointing record of the space shuttle left the United States with little ability to even carry components of SDI into space. A decade after the president unveiled the scheme, it remained a distant prospect.

The Cold War Intensifies

The Soviets denounced Reagan as a warmonger, suspended arms control negotiations, but failed to mount an effective response to American initiatives. Now old and decrepit, Communist Party chief Leonid Brezhnev, in power since 1964, presided over a lethargic and corrupt government. Following his death, in 1982, his aging colleagues groped for a successor. The oligarchy selected KGB chief Yuri Andropov to serve as General Secretary. Although reputed to support reforms, Andropov suffered from kidney disease and spent most of his brief term on a dialysis machine. Following his death in 1984, the party elders tapped as their leader a lackluster timeserver, Konstantin Chernenko. Already sick with emphysema, he survived one year. When asked about his reluctance to hold a summit with a Soviet leader, Reagan quipped "they keep dying on me." Only in 1985, when the 54-year-old Mikhail Gorbachev emerged as General Secretary of the Communist Party, did the Soviet Union once again have an effective leader.

Meanwhile, two events provided Reagan with ample opportunity to launch his anti-communist barbs. In December 1981, as the Solidarity labor movement in Poland threatened to sweep away the Soviet-supported Communist regime, Moscow pushed the Polish army to impose martial law. Reagan accused Moscow of unleashing the "forces of tyranny" against a peaceful neighbor and called on Americans to light "candles of freedom" in support of the Poles.

Two years later, in September 1983, a tragic error by Soviet air force commanders angered Americans even more. Apparently, a series of navigational mistakes caused Korean Air Lines flight #007 to stray far off course en route from Alaska to Seoul. It flew for some distance over Soviet territory, including a secret missile test site. Just before it exited Soviet air space, a Soviet fighter pilot shot down the airliner, killing all 269 people on board, including a member of Congress.

Reagan denounced this as an "act of barbarism," directed "against the world and the moral precepts which guide human relations among people everywhere." Soviet leaders, he insisted, deliberately and callously destroyed a civilian aircraft without warning. The evidence, however, did not fully support the president's contention. American electronic intercepts of Soviet communications showed that local air defense commanders did not at first realize they were tracking a civilian airliner. They thought an American RC-135 spy plane, which had earlier flown near Soviet air space, had returned to spy upon the missile range. (In 1991 the Soviet pilot asserted that before firing he knew the target was a 747 jet, but believed it was carrying out a spy mission and had refused to respond to warnings.) The tragic shootdown of the airliner probably resulted more from mistaken identity than premeditated murder. Reagan and other top officials learned of these facts shortly after their initial remarks. They declined, however, to amend their conclusions since, as the president later admitted, the incident "gave badly needed impetus in Congress to the rearmament programs and postponed . . . attempts to gut our efforts to restore American military might."

The administration's emotional rhetoric as well as the inability of Moscow's doddering leadership to explain its action, buoyed Reagan's image as an uncompromising critic of evil and bolstered congressional support for his defense program. Because so few people, in or out of government, understood the technical complexities of modern weapons systems, little informed debate took place. Most Americans were uncertain how large or expensive an arsenal they needed. Did security in the nuclear age require equality with or superiority over the Soviet Union? In many cases, Congress, journalists, and the public debated marginal details of defense policy rather than the overall logic of the buying spree.

The Pentagon spent so much money during Reagan's first term that contractors had great difficulty manufacturing all the ships, tanks, planes, and missiles ordered. The resulting price inflation meant that despite the near doubling of procurement budgets, only about 25% more large-ticket items were acquired. The enormous increase also encouraged a wave of corruption. Many weapons rushed into production with inadequate testing failed to meet specifications.

The B-1 and B-2 bombers, replacements for the venerable B-52, first deployed in the mid-1950s, cost over $200 million and $800 million respectively per plane. Neither performed as promised. The B-2, or stealth, had an especially embarrassing problem: it appeared on radar screens when it was not supposed to. Yet what citizen could gauge if these were fair prices or if performance problems merited tough criticism? Journalists and members of Congress expressed outrage over reports contractors charged $500 for each of the toilet seats and hammers carried on these aircraft. Everyone knew the fair cost for such items and recognized price gouging. But who could say what the air force should pay for a stealth bomber? Critics in and out of government often denounced contractors for profiteering on small items while ignoring more serious procurement problems.

As Reagan completed his second term, the Justice Department announced that a secret probe, code-named "Ill Wind," had resulted in the indictment of numerous Defense Department officials, private consultants, and defense contractors. Among other things, they had colluded to rig bidding procedures and fake quality control tests on billions of dollars worth of equipment. As of 1991, 51 individuals and companies had been convicted. Congress passed new procurement regulations in 1988 and stiffened restrictions on Pentagon officials taking defense industry jobs immediately after leaving government service.

America and the World

Terrorism

President Reagan and leading members of his administration described terrorism in the Middle East and elsewhere as among the gravest threats to the United States and its allies. In a speech delivered on January 21, 1981, the day after Reagan took office, Secretary of State Alexander Haig linked the Soviet Union to all of the world's terrorism. When the State Department's Bureau of Intelligence and Research issued a secret report casting doubt on this judgment, Haig and CIA director Casey took issue with it.

Casey went so far as to call the authors into his office for a dressing down. He waved before them a copy of journalist Claire Sterling's book, *The Terror Network*, which argued that Moscow was, indeed, responsible for the bulk of the world's terrorism. This argument did not impress most of the career intelligence analysts, however. They recognized many of Sterling's findings as a repetition of their own anti-communist "black propaganda" planted in Europe by the CIA to discredit the Soviet Union.

Nevertheless, Casey's enthusiasm for Sterling's conclusions remained high. When the journalist published another book in 1984 (*The Time of the Assassins*), the spy chief accepted her claim that the Soviet KGB had masterminded the 1981 attempt by a Turk to assassinate Pope John Paul II. Allegedly, Moscow hoped to demoralize a restive Poland by killing the Polish-born Pope. Even though the CIA had concluded in a 1983 study that no firm evidence linked the Soviets to the plot, Casey and his deputy, Robert M. Gates, ordered preparation of a new study in 1985 that portrayed Moscow as masterminding the assassination attempt. Interestingly, Casey pushed hard for this report at the time when reformer Mikhail Gorbachev had come to power and was seeking to improve relations with the Reagan administration.

In spite of efforts to reduce the phenomenon of terrorism to a Soviet plot, terrorism in the Middle East and elsewhere was generally a symptom, not a source, of regional violence and often an act of desperation. Some observers described it as the atomic bomb of the weak. Nevertheless, the media played up the often ghastly consequences of terrorism and the American public interpreted the government's inability to prevent or retaliate against such outrages as a sign of national impotence.

Even one of the president's most vivid declarations on terrorism, Oliver North revealed, was a product of media hype. In October 1985 American F-14 jets intercepted and forced to land in Sicily an EgyptAir plane carrying PLO terrorist Abul Abbas who had just masterminded the hijacking of the Italian ocean liner *Achille Lauro* during which American passenger Leon Klinghoffer had been brutally killed. As North and Pat Buchanan worked on a statement, they received a call from *New York Post* editor Niles Latham. "We need a great headline," Latham said. "We'd like to use 'You Can Run But You Can't Hide.' " The two staffers had Reagan read the statement, allowing the *Post* to scoop the competition. The euphoria proved premature, however, since the Italian government promptly released the suspect.

The kidnapping of a handful of Americans in Lebanon, occasional aircraft and ship hijackings, and the bombing of airliners, while inexcusable, were marginal acts in the world arena. In aggregate, during the 1980s, about as many American civilians were killed by lightning while playing golf than died at the hands of terrorists. Terrorism became a popular obsession partly because President Reagan made it so.

The Middle East

Like all his predecessors since 1945, Reagan tried and failed to impose American solutions to Middle Eastern problems. Civil strife in Lebanon and Afghanistan, a war between Iran and Iraq, and a continuing cycle of violence between Israel and its Arab neighbors frustrated numerous attempts at mediation. At the outset of the new administration, Secretary of State Haig tried to convince Israel and conservative Arab states (Saudi Arabia, Jordan, Egypt) to join an American-brokered alliance aimed against Soviet influence in the region. These nations welcomed American aid, but preferred to use it against local rivals, not the Soviet Union.

In June 1982, Haig encouraged the invasion of Lebanon by the Israeli army to destroy Palestinian Liberation Organization (PLO) forces that controlled part of that country. But when Israel put Beirut under siege, Michael Deaver and National Security Adviser William P. Clark raised objections. Deaver even threatened to resign unless Reagan pressed the Israeli government to stop bombing Beirut. Clark contacted PLO representatives in an effort to negotiate a compromise. Haig, already on bad terms with Reagan's inner circle, quit in a huff. The president then appointed George P. Shultz, who had served President Nixon as budget director and Secretary of Labor, to head the State Department. He labored mightily for six years to bring some semblance of order to American policy.

By August, the United States arranged for the evacuation from Lebanon of the same PLO forces it had previously hoped to see eradicated. Reagan and Shultz urged that Israel allow the PLO to establish a homeland on the west bank of the Jordan River in return for guarantees of peace with the Jewish state. Neither Israel nor the Palestinians agreed. Meanwhile, the assassination of Christian Lebanese leader Bashir Gemayal on September 14 sparked Christian massacres, tacitly encouraged by the Israelis, of Palestinians in two Beirut refugee camps.

As the chaotic Lebanese political scene approached complete anarchy, the United States, France, and Italy sent peacekeeping forces to Beirut. They were intended to bolster Christian forces and to counterbalance the presence of Syrian army and Shi'ite Muslim and Druse military units, each of which dominated parts of the fragile country. But Lebanese Muslims bitterly resented Western aid to the Christian minority. On April 18, 1983, a suicide squad attacked the American embassy in Beirut, killing 63 people.

In retaliation, the battleship *New Jersey,* sailing off Lebanon, shelled Shi'ite and Druse positions. This further antagonized Muslim forces and provoked a desperate act of revenge. On October 23 a terrorist drove a truck filled with explosives into Marine barracks near Beirut's airport, killing 241 Marines. French troops were attacked simultaneously.

President Reagan offered a moving tribute to the slaughtered young men, but failed to offer any coherent explanation of what American interest they had died defending. In his 1984 State of the Union Address, he declared that keeping the Marines in Lebanon was "central to our credibility on a global scale." But two weeks later the president ordered the troops out of Beirut. Lebanese factions promptly resumed their communal slaughter. Reagan's later assertion, that he "didn't appreciate fully enough the depth of hatred and the complexity of the problems that make the Middle East such a jungle" rang flat.

The problem of Palestinian refugees and those living under Israeli occupation also defied an American solution. Beginning in December 1987, Palestinians in territory occupied by Israel since 1967 began an *intifada,* or civilian uprising against Israeli authorities. Israeli troops and police responded harshly, killing some 800 Palestinians over the next three years.

In 1988, after decades of rejecting Israel's legitimacy, Palestinian leader Yassir Arafat responded to American suggestions by declaring the PLO accepted Israel's right to exist. United States diplomats then began a cautious dialogue with that organization. However, neither Arafat nor Israeli leaders agreed on terms for establishment of a Palestinian state acceptable to Israel. Washington's close ties to Israel complicated negotiations with Arab leaders who doubted American evenhandedness.

Libya

Libya's demagogic strongman, Colonel Muammar Qaddafi, emerged as the Reagan administration's favorite villain in the Middle East. Bloated with cash from oil deposits, Qaddafi pursued an ambitious plan to modernize his country of fewer than three million people. Much of his wealth bought Soviet military hardware and some bankrolled various terrorist groups operating in the Middle East and Europe. The Libyan's flamboyant, aggressive style and personal insults directed toward American leaders particularly outraged Reagan. The president called Qaddafi a "mad clown" and charged that the Libyan leader hired assassins to kill him.

Anxious, as George Shultz phrased it, to "put Qaddafi back in his box," Washington deployed a naval flotilla in the Gulf of Sidra, on Libya's northern coast. Libya claimed the gulf as territorial waters and its forces clashed several times with the Americans as Qaddafi dared them to cross the "line of death." Reagan authorized American ships and planes to conduct "hot pursuit" against Libyan aircraft that might harass them. When an admiral asked the president how far they could pursue, Reagan shot back, "all the way into the hangar." United States and Libyan jets fought air duels over the Gulf of Sidra in 1981 and again in 1988, resulting in the loss of several Libyan planes and ships.

In April 1986, Libyan agents were implicated in the bombing of a Berlin night club frequented by American soldiers. Reagan, calling Qaddafi the "mad dog of the Middle East," ordered a retaliatory air attack on Tripoli, and specifically against Qaddafi's compound. The raid failed to eliminate the colonel although it killed one of his daughters.

Qaddafi remained a bitter critic of the United States but tempered his violence against American allies and interests. "After the attack on Tripoli," Reagan explained, "we didn't hear much more from Qaddafi's terrorists." Not only American retaliation, but the steep decline of oil prices after 1986 and Libya's wars with its North African neighbors probably restrained Qaddafi.

The Persian Gulf

The bloody nine-year war between Iraq and Iran, for control of deep water ports, territory, and regional influence, fought from 1980 to 1988, claimed the lives of almost two million people. Choosing sides was difficult. Washington feared the expansionist goals and Soviet ties of Iraqi leader Saddam Hussein nearly as much as the Islamic fundamentalism promoted by Iran's Ayatollah Khomeini. American experts worried that a victory by either country would result in its domination of much of the oil-rich Persian Gulf region.

To prevent this, the United States played two hands. It provided secret military aid and intelligence to whichever side appeared to be losing the war at any given time. This, it was hoped, would produce a stalemate that tied down both regimes. From 1981 to 1986, Washington generally provided assistance to Iran. Some support went to Iraq after 1982 and the aid increased after 1986. This policy was sometimes coordinated with Israel. The Jewish state, more fearful of nearby Iraq and concerned for the safety of some

80,000 Iranian Jews, generally assisted Iran. During 1981–82, the United States and Israel secretly sold Iran several billion dollars worth of American military equipment.

In 1987, when Iran appeared on the verge of victory, Washington abruptly expanded aid to the Iraqis. Iran responded by attacking western oil tankers carrying Iraqi cargo in the Persian Gulf. Reagan ordered the Navy to escort ships carrying petroleum, resulting in several small clashes with the Iranians. The bloodiest incidents of the undeclared war in the gulf involved cases of mistaken identity. In May 1987, an Iraqi pilot, confusing the destroyer U.S.S. *Stark* for an Iranian ship, attacked it with a missile that killed 37 sailors. A year later, the captain of the U.S.S. *Vincennes* mistakenly shot down an Iranian passenger plane killing 290 civilians. (In retaliation, Iranian, Syrian, or Libyan agents placed a bomb on a December 1988 Pan Am flight from London, killing 270 people.)

During the war, Iraq used poison gas against domestic rebels, such as the Kurds, as well as Iranian troops. Saddam Hussein also pursued efforts to build an atomic bomb. Nevertheless, the Reagan administration considered Iraq a useful counterforce to Iran and hoped to woo Saddam Hussein by providing critical technology and assistance. American, French, and German aid to Iraq only encouraged Saddam Hussein's megalomania and probably convinced him he had a free hand to dominate weaker neighbors like Kuwait. In 1988, however, both Iran and Iraq were exhausted by their inclusive war. That August they signed a cease-fire but maintained their conflicting claims.

Afghanistan

The Soviet invasion of Afghanistan in 1979, the first time since 1945 the Kremlin had used its regular armed forces outside Eastern Europe, aroused anger and fear in the West. Brezhnev and his two successors justified this as "fraternal" help to a communist government under siege. In fact, the Kremlin intervened to save an unpopular pro-Soviet regime threatened by a coalition of anticommunist guerrillas, or *mujahidin*. Many of the guerrillas were Islamic fundamentalists who admired the Ayatollah Khomeini, America's sworn enemy. Despite this, both Presidents Carter and

Reagan feared the Soviets would use Afghanistan as an avenue to dominate the oil resources of the Persian Gulf.

The Reagan administration expanded American support to the *mujahidin*. The CIA provided weapons, training, and economic assistance to the guerrillas, using neighboring Pakistan as a base of operations. As the fighting mounted, millions of Afghans fled the country, most resettling in Pakistan.

At first, the fiercely committed but lightly armed guerrillas proved no match for the Soviet invaders. When the CIA made shoulder-fired anti-aircraft missiles available, the *mujahidin* neutralized the invader's air advantage. Members of the Reagan administration often described the struggle as the Soviets' Vietnam, a curious analogy to make given Reagan's description of that earlier war as America's "noble cause."

The inability of Soviet forces to crush the rebels, despite a decade of struggle, bore some similarity to the war in Southeast Asia. Faced with mounting casualties, costs, and public grumbling, Moscow's new leader, Mikhail Gorbachev, decided to cut his losses. Like President Nixon in Vietnam, he sought a "peace with honor" on the best terms he could get. In 1988 Gorbachev blamed the costly and unpopular invasion on his dead predecessors and ordered Soviet forces out of Afghanistan.

Peace, unfortunately, remained elusive. Soviet forces withdrew from combat, although Moscow continued giving aid and advice to its supporters in Kabul. The United States also maintained an arms pipeline to the guerrillas. However, without a foreign enemy present to unify their ranks, the *mujahidin* fell into factional disputes. The Soviet-backed regime in Kabul proved difficult to dislodge.

The New Banana Wars

Obsessed with what it perceived as the Soviet threat to the Western hemisphere and eager to erase the memory of humiliation in Vietnam, the Reagan administration revived the old tradition of American muscle flexing in Latin America. The United States invaded one country (Grenada), financed civil wars in two (El Salvador and

Nicaragua), and used economic pressure in an effort to topple the government in another (Panama).

Administration rhetoric about the nature of the Red Peril often sounded like a throwback to the early years of the Cold War. State Department and CIA officials spoke about a "Moscow-Havana" axis whose Soviet-supplied Cuban agents spread revolution throughout Latin America. Shortly after Reagan entered the White House, UN ambassador Jeane Kirkpatrick informed a group of conservative fund raisers that Central America and the Caribbean had become "the most important place in the world for us." America's ability to exercise global influence and confront the Soviet Union, she explained, depended on "not having to devote the lion's share of our attention and our resources to the defense of ourselves in our own hemisphere." By creating puppet regimes in Central America, the president warned, Moscow and Havana planned to choke off America's "lifeline to the outside world." Reagan also raised the fear that revolutions in the region would drive millions of poor refugees ("leftbacks," a journalist quipped) north to destabilize the United States.

Critics, like Senator Christopher Dodd, a Connecticut Democrat, countered that Reagan and his advisers knew "as much about Central America in 1983 as we knew about Indochina in 1963." As a former Peace Corps volunteer in Latin America, Dodd argued that "if Central America were not racked with poverty, there would be no revolution."

The administration tried to win public backing for a more assertive policy by assembling a commission on Central America chaired by former Secretary of State Henry Kissinger. The commission's 1984 report noted the social and economic roots of the region's problems and admitted that Moscow could not be blamed for everything. Although it endorsed more economic aid, the Kissinger panel stressed the need to fund the military in El Slavador and the anti-communist guerrillas in Nicaragua.

Reagan had surprising difficulty persuading Congress or the public to see the dangers he or his commission described. Most citizens found it doubtful that the future of Western civilization depended on who ruled in Managua or Tegucigalpa. In spite of the president's continuing efforts to arouse passion on the subject, polls taken throughout the 1980s revealed that three-fourths of the public did not know or care what groups the United States favored or opposed in Central America. A large majority of respondents opposed sending troops to the region, even to stop communist takeovers.

El Salvador

Frustrated by his inability to build a consensus behind an interventionist policy, the president relied on a combination of military aid and covert warfare in Central America. The Reagan administration spent nearly five billion dollars providing military and economic aid to El Salvador between 1981 and 1989. A terribly poor country in which 2% of the people controlled nearly all wealth, El Salvador had been racked by rebellions throughout the century. Since 1979, a civilian regime, headed by Christian Democrat Jose Napoleon Duarte, nominally ruled. But the right-wing military held real power.

A coalition of leftist guerrillas, based in both rural and urban areas, mounted a major challenge to the government. The United States provided the Salvadoran army with massive aid, but the military could not quash the rebellion. The army squandered much of the money and used the arms to wage a fierce campaign of repression against civilians suspected of sympathizing with the rebels or agitating for social change. Army "death squads" killed as many as 70,000 peasants, teachers, union organizers, and church workers. Robert D'Aubuisson, a former army officer and founder of the right-wing ARENA Party, was widely judged responsible for this terrorism. Some U.S. politicians, like North Carolina Republican Senator Jesse Helms, praised D'Aubuisson even after his assassins killed several American church workers and union organizers.

Many Americans recoiled from this slaughter. Congress opposed direct intervention but hesitated to tie the hands of an otherwise popular president. It did limit the number of U.S. military advisers stationed in El Salvador to under 100 and insisted that Reagan periodically certify that "progress" had occurred in curbing human rights abuses by the Salvadoran military. So long as the president issued a positive finding, he had authority to continue military and economic aid.

After eight years of bloodshed, the Salvadoran government had neither defeated the guerrillas nor carried out promised reforms. In 1988 Duarte and his followers lost an election to the right-wing ARENA party. The war, and civilian deaths, continued.

Grenada

American military intervention in Grenada followed a very different course than elsewhere in Latin America. The Reagan administration achieved a quick, effective, and popular military victory over a group of thugs. A tiny island and former British colony, Grenada had been ruled by a Marxist, Maurice Bishop, since 1979. Although the United States suspended economic aid to his government in 1981, it seemed too insignificant an irritant to bother the administration. Some tourists continued to visit the rustic island, although the lack of a modern airport hindered travel. The main American presence consisted of several hundred medical students enrolled in the St. George's University School of Medicine, a for-profit institution that attracted aspiring physicians unable to gain admission to mainland institutions.

The Bishop regime proclaimed its solidarity with Cuba's Fidel Castro and the Marxist Sandinistas in Nicaragua. A contingent of several hundred armed Cuban construction workers labored on the island building an airport that Prime Minister Bishop called a boon to tourism and Washington labeled a potential Cuban or Soviet air base.

On October 12, 1983, a militant faction of the Marxist New Jewel movement, led by Gen. Hudson Austin, overthrew Bishop who had recently softened his anti-Yankee rhetoric. Austin murdered Bishop, imposed martial law, and announced a strict curfew. Still, the coup did not seem to affect American interests. Nevertheless, President Reagan ordered the Pentagon to prepare an invasion force to rescue the American students.

Then, on October 23, a terrorist attack in Beirut killed 241 marines. Unable to identify the perpetrators or use its vast military power to exact revenge, the Reagan administration felt intense frustration. Seemingly as an afterthought amid the confusion, the president's advisers recalled the American medical students in Grenada. Although none had been harmed or were known to face danger, administration officials considered their safety sufficiently in doubt to warrant intervention. Perhaps the dramatic rescue of potential American hostages would divert attention from the carnage in Beirut. After consulting with the leaders of a few tiny Caribbean islands whom Washington ignored before and ever since, on October 25 the president ordered thousands of marines and army troops to storm ashore and liberate Grenada from what Reagan called a "brutal gang of thugs."

The invasion met only limited resistance from Hudson's small band of followers. The Cubans fought a bit harder. Although the president described the operation as a "textbook success," numerous logistic problems delayed for several days full control of the island. The Pentagon had equipped naval, army, and air force units with incompatible radios. To speak to the ships offshore, one soldier used a public phone to call Washington. The Pentagon then patched him through to the naval flotilla. Lacking accurate maps, invading troops relied on tourist brochures. Amid the confusion, the attackers accidentally shelled an insane asylum, which accounted for most of the few dozen Grenadian casualties. Nineteen Americans died, and over a hundred suffered wounds. Despite its occasional similarity to a Gilbert and Sullivan operetta, the Pentagon handed out an unprecedented 8,000 medals to men in the invading force.

Reagan reported that the Cubans had stockpiled thousands of weapons on the island, enough to equip an army of terrorists. He placed special emphasis on a letter discovered from a Soviet general to a Grenadian commander that lavished praise on the island as the "third outpost of Communism in the New world—after Cuba and Nicaragua." El Salvador, he predicted, would soon become the fourth. The president believed this confirmed the Soviet master plan to dominate the hemisphere.

In the invasion's aftermath, a letter from an army helicopter pilot to the White House struck an especially responsive chord in Reagan. The pilot pointed out that Grenada produced half the world's nutmeg. If the Soviets had taken over the island, they would have "controlled much of the world's nutmeg supply." Since "you can't make an eggnog without nutmeg," he pointed out to the president, and since "some people would say you can't have

Christmas without an eggnog," the "Russians were trying to steal Christmas. We stopped them."

Many Grenadians welcomed the Americans as saviors who might bring peace and prosperity to their island. Free elections restored representative government but Washington rapidly lost interest and failed to fund promised development programs. Grenada returned to its normal poverty and obscurity, searching in vain for a benefactor to complete its modern airport.

News blackouts and censorship prevented the public from learning about invasion snafus. Most Americans were thrilled that the United States had "won one for a change." Scenes of returned medical students falling to their knees and kissing American soil diverted attention from the statement by the school director that the students had never been in danger. Reagan's campaign staff in 1984 used footage of the grateful students, with devastating effect, in the political campaign against Walter Mondale, the Democratic nominee, who initially condemned the invasion as a violation of international law.

The celebration of victory in Grenada coincided with a wave of boisterous nationalism that Reagan both stimulated and rode. During the 1980s several popular adventure films and novels portrayed American heroes who exacted revenge in Vietnam, defeated Soviet troops, and crushed Third World upstarts. In his series of *Rocky* and *Rambo* films, actor-director Sylvester Stallone beat Russian and North Vietnamese soldiers to a bloody pulp. Kung-fu champion Chuck Norris kick-boxed his way through Southeast Asia to rescue American prisoners abandoned by their government. In the film *Top Gun*, gallant American fliers shot Libyan and Soviet pilots out of the sky with a grin and a swagger. Tom Clancy's bestselling novel *The Hunt for Red October* portrayed an American victory over the Soviet navy. In these and other films and novels, a character plaintively asks "Are we gonna be allowed to win this time?"

The drive to "win" took on special meaning during the 1984 Olympics held in Los Angeles. Partly because of a Soviet bloc boycott, American athletes triumphed in a large number of events. Crowds waved banners proclaiming "We're #1" and chanted "U.S.A., U.S.A." Television coverage sometimes skipped victory ceremonies in which non-Americans took top honors and often declined to broadcast the national anthems of other teams. The Reagan re-election campaign included much Olympic footage in its TV spots.

Reagan's landslide victory over Walter Mondale in November 1984 prompted House Speaker Tip O'Neill to tell the president: "In my fifty years in public life, I've never seen a man more popular than you with the American people." Before the election, poll takers had detected some voter anxiety over Reagan's bellicose rhetoric. To allay these fears, the president's aides softened his campaign remarks about the Soviet Union and Central America. After victory, Reagan struck a positive tone, declaring that in his second term he would push arms control. "I have no more important goal," he stated, then "reducing and ultimately eliminating nuclear weapons."

When National Security Adviser Robert McFarlane asked him to select from a long list, including such complicated issues as arms control, the Arab-Israeli conflict, proxy wars in the Third World, etc., a few foreign policy goals to pursue over the next four years, Reagan beamed, "Let's do them all!"

Reagan, as his advisers knew, paid close attention to only a handful of issues. In foreign policy, none engaged him more than assisting the anti-communist *Contra* guerrillas in Nicaragua. In a typical speech, delivered in 1986, he described the Sandinista government as a "second Libya right on the doorsteps" of America, a "safe-house, a command post for international terror." "Could there be," he asked, "any greater tragedy than for us to sit back and permit this cancer to spread?" Who, hearing this alarm, imagined that the president forging links to Iran was Reagan.

6

The Iran-Contra Affair and
the "End" of the Cold War

D URING THE 1980 election campaign, Reagan had criticized Jimmy
Carter for abandoning America's long-term client, Nicaraguan director Anastasio Somoza, whose family had ruled that
country as a personal fiefdom since the 1920s. After 1981, the new
president accused the Sandinista leadership of turning Nicaragua
into a "Soviet ally on the American mainland." In one especially
vivid speech, Reagan conjured up a vision of Sandinistas driving a
convoy of armed pick-up trucks north into Harlingen, Texas, a
small town along the Mexican border. Political satirist Garry Tru-
deau parodied the warning in his "Doonesbury" comic strip which
depicted a group of "good ole' boys" from Harlingen peering
through the sights of their hunting rifles ready to repulse the pend-
ing invasion.

The Sandinistas, to be sure, were real Marxists who bitterly criticized the United States for its long support of Somoza. They did
receive aid from the Soviet Union and other anti-American governments. Also, as Reagan charged, they failed to hold free elections,
stifled dissent, socialized parts of the economy, and served as a
conduit of arms (many of them U.S. weapons captured by North
Vietnam in 1975) from the Soviet bloc to the Salvadoran guerrillas.

These sins, however, had to be seen in perspective. Sandinista
human rights abuses paled before the gory record of pro-American
regimes in El Salvador and Guatemala. Since the entire population

of Nicaragua numbered less than that in some neighborhoods in Mexico City, Reagan's talk of the grave threat posed by the Sandinistas to the entire hemisphere was highly exaggerated. Also, in 1989, *after* the United States abandoned military efforts to depose the Sandinistas, they permitted free elections and allowed their victorious opponents to form a democratic government.

Shortly after becoming president in 1981, Reagan instructed CIA director William Casey to organize anti-Sandinista guerrillas among Nicaraguan exiles. In order to distance the United States from this activity, initially the CIA relied on members of the Argentine armed forces to conduct the training. But in 1982 Great Britain and Argentina fought a brief but fierce war over control of the Falkland Islands, a bleak British colony in the South Atlantic claimed by Argentina. Furious at Washington for its support of Britain, the Argentines quit helping and left the program in American hands.

Thereafter, the *contras,* or, as Reagan called them, "freedom fighters," survived almost entirely on United States aid. Much of it still arrived indirectly. For example, between 1981 and 1986, Panamanian dictator General Manuel Noriega served as a conduit for American money and arms to the *contras*. He conferred several times between 1981 and 1986 with William Casey, Vice President George Bush, and National Security Council staff member Col. Oliver North to arrange details of the aid operation.

Noriega, whose sole motivation appears to have been personal enrichment, demanded a price for his services. As the Reagan administration already knew, the Panamanian strongman had gone into business with Colombian drug smugglers, including members of the infamous Medellin cocaine cartel, who used Panama to transship narcotics to the U.S. market and launder their money. Even as Reagan declared a "war on drugs," his administration overlooked these sins in return for Noriega's cooperation in the American-directed program to help the *contras*. In the view of former ambassador to Costa Rica Francis J. McNeil, the Reagan administration "coddled General Noriega in the interests of Nicaraguan policy." Similarly, the administration tolerated reported drug smuggling by the Hondurian military and even among the *contras* themselves, all in the name of anti-communism. The president lost no opportunity, however, to highlight reports of Cuban and Sandinista involvement in drug smuggling.

By 1987–88, public disclosure of illegal American support for the *contras,* the death of William Casey, and the move toward a negotiated settlement in Nicaragua reduced Noriega's usefulness to Washington. As his links to Washington became a public embarrassment, the Reagan administration in February 1988 permitted the Justice Department to indict him on drug smuggling charges and imposed economic sanctions on Panama. At the end of 1989, President Bush ordered U.S. forces to invade the isthmus. Seized and taken to stand trial in Miami (the case came to court only in September 1991), the ex-dictator maintained that his involvement with drug traffickers had taken place with the knowledge and tacit approval of American officials as part of the anti-*contra* program.

With American support, *contra* ranks swelled to between ten and twenty thousand men by 1985. Some *contra* political leaders were real democrats who had opposed Somoza. But most of the military commanders, the real power in the movement, had served in the deposed dictator's army.

When members of Congress raised questions about the scope and purpose of covert operations in Nicaragua, CIA director Casey assured them that neither the Reagan administration nor the *contras* sought to overthrow the Sandinista regime. Instead, the spy agency used the guerrillas to interdict Sandinista military aid to rebels in El Salvador. But Congress grew restive over mounting evidence that *contra* attacks within Nicaragua had killed thousands of civilians. Representative Edward P. Boland, a Democrat from Massachusetts, sponsored a resolution in 1982, known as the Boland Amendment, which capped CIA aid to the *contras* at $24 million and ordered that none of the funds be used to topple the Nicaraguan government.

Reagan, who dubbed Congress a meddlesome "committee of 535" members, rejected the notion of legislative oversight of his foreign policy initiatives. He directed his subordinates to circumvent the law. The Pentagon undermined the $24 million spending cap by providing, at little or no cost, supposedly surplus weapons to the guerrillas. The CIA prepared a booklet on ways to assassinate Sandinista officials and also coordinated attacks on Nicaraguan ports and transport facilities. These acts violated the Boland Amendment as well as the promises William Casey had made to members of Congress.

In April 1984, a story in the *Wall Street Journal* revealed that CIA personnel had mined Nicaraguan harbors, violating Casey's assurance to the Senate Select Committee on Intelligence that the agency would avoid direct military involvement. This infuriated the committee chair, venerable and conservative Barry Goldwater, who noted that the CIA's actions violated international law. In an angry letter to Casey, the Arizona Republican wrote that the issue "gets down to one, little, simple phrase: I am pissed off." In response, Casey and the president both promised the Senate Intelligence Committee that they would keep it informed about all future covert actions of an important nature. As it turned out, the administration did no such thing.

Shortly after appointing Alan Fiers to head the CIA's Central American task force, Casey told him the Soviet Union was "tremendously overextended and vulnerable." If America challenged the Soviets everywhere and defeated them in even one place "that will shatter the mythology . . . and it will all start to unravel." "Nick-a-wog-wah," as Casey pronounced it, "is that place." Fiers and CIA associate Duane R. Clarridge worked tirelessly to train and support the *contras*.

In October 1984, when the initial funds allocated for the *contras* ran out, Congress moved to forbid further direct or indirect assistance by passing a stricter version of the Boland Amendment. "Boland II," as it was known, barred the CIA or "any other agency or entity involved in intelligence activities" from aiding the guerrillas. Congressman Boland called the prohibition "air tight with no exceptions." Speaker Tip O'Neill proclaimed that the *contras* were "dead."

The obituary proved premature. National Security Adviser Robert McFarlane and his chief deputy, Admiral John Poindexter, understood that the president "wanted to be sure that the *contras* were supported." They placed Oliver North in charge of plans to "hold them together," as North put it, "in body and soul." After conferring with Casey, McFarlane, and Poindexter, North devised a scheme to "privatize" *contra* aid by raising funds from foreign governments and private citizens. He opened a numbered Swiss bank account for the rebels and induced several pro-American governments, including Israel, South Africa, Saudi Arabia, Brunei, South Korea, and Taiwan to make small contributions to the guerrilla force in return for American goodwill or surreptitious repayment in the guise of other projects. National Security Adviser McFarlane later testified he kept Reagan, Vice President Bush, Secretary of State George Shultz, and Defense Secretary Caspar Weinberger well informed. At a meeting of the National Security Council in June 1984, attended by the above-named officials, Shultz admonished Reagan that his order to circumvent Congress by soliciting foreign funds might constitute an "impeachable offense." The president must have taken the warning seriously because the minutes of the meeting recorded him as saying that if the story ever got out "we'll all be hanging by our thumbs in front of the White House."

The Rise of Oliver North

Marine Lt. Col. Oliver North, a decorated veteran of the Vietnam War, acted as the key intermediary in the secret projects linking arms sales to Iran and support for the *contras*. He joined the NSC early in the Reagan administration on the recommendation of his friend, National Security Adviser and fellow Marine, Robert McFarlane. Although North's nearly manic devotion to duty impressed many superiors, Michael Deaver worried about his influence on the president and he added the name of the NSC staffer to those who should be kept "out of Reagan's office because he was dangerous." Speechwriter Peggy Noonan described North as a true believer who "had the sunny, undimmed confidence of a man who lacks insight into his own weaknesses."

After he left office, Ronald Reagan claimed he "knew Oliver North only slightly" and never met privately with him until "his last day at the NSC." Despite overwhelming evidence that the colonel carried out the president's plans, Reagan later sought to distance himself from North by insisting "I hardly knew him." The president may not have held intimate working meetings with North (and the colonel did tend to embellish his familiarity with Reagan and other luminaries), but the over 50,000 pages of depositions taken after the scandal broke made it clear that McFarlane, Poindexter, and North all took their orders from the Oval Office. The president may not have known or cared about details of the NSC operations, but he issued the marching orders. As North later put it, "the president didn't always know what he knew." When Reagan asked for ways to get around the Boland Amendment, for example, North persuaded him that the prohibition only barred the CIA, not the White House or NSC staff, from helping the *contras.*

While North and others on the NSC staff went forward soliciting funds from foreign governments and private donors, the president again asked Congress to appropriate $14 million in "humanitarian aid" for the guerrillas. Congress spurned the request in a vote in April 1985. Right after this vote, however, the Sandinista leader, Daniel Ortega, flew to Moscow to express solidarity with the Soviets. His visit embarrassed and angered enough members of Congress so that in June they reversed themselves and approved $24 million in non-lethal *contra* aid. Still, North complained angrily, "You can't win a war with blankets and band-aids."

Oliver North and William Casey—despite the admitted prohibition on CIA involvement—worked to expand the private network of those helping the anti-communist guerrillas. Casey urged expanding the operation to create what North later dubbed "the Enterprise," a covert force "you could pull off the shelf and use at a moment's notice" without congressional funding or oversight. North hired retired Air Force General Richard Secord and an Iranian-American arms dealer, Albert Hakim, to buy weapons with private funds deposited in Swiss banks.

Although denied at the time and for several years after the revelation of the secret supply network, a number of high level CIA officials, besides Director Casey, cooperated with Colonel North. From 1984 through 1986, Alan D. Fiers, head of the agency's Central American task force, and Claire George, the number-three man in the intelligence heirarchy who, as Deputy Director of Operations supervised clandestine operations, met with North and retired General Richard Secord to coordinate secret arms shipments. Some of these meetings took place in the White House, suggesting the close connection of the president to what transpired. In addition, the Assistant Scretary of State for Latin America, Elliott Abrams, worked closely with North to support the *contras*.

In addition to the contributions from friendly foreign governments, North cultivated donations from wealthy Americans. He utilized the talents of Republican Party fund raiser, Carl "Spitz" Channel, a gay conservative whose cadre of handsome young men were assigned to "romance" rich widows, whom he and North mockingly called the "blue haired ladies," on behalf of the *contras*. The donations were falsely called tax deductible.

Typically, North narrated a slide show before an individual or small group. The potential donors saw pictures of *contras* in heroic poses and of military hardware such as helicopters, rifles, and mortars with pricetags. The colonel then left the room to avoid technical complicity in illegal fund raising or violation of the neutrality act. Channel then requested donations. As a special reward, North offered major donors short audiences with Ronald Reagan who later met several of the benefactors. "Project Democracy," the code name for this part of the operation, raised several million dollars during 1985. Three of its biggest contributors included Joseph Coors, Nelson Bunker Hunt, and Ellen Clayton Garwood. Appreciative *contras* painted a Coors beer logo on the tail of one of their aircraft.

The Iranian Connection

The *contra* aid program merged with Middle East policy partly by design, partly by accident. On June 14, 1985, Lebanese Shi'ite terrorists hijacked a TWA flight in Athens and flew it to Beirut. The highjackers executed a navy enlisted man travelling as a passenger, then threatened to kill 39 other Americans on board unless Israel released 700 Lebanese prisoners it held. Reagan denounced this extortion, promising never to bargain with terrorists. Privately, however, he urged the Israelis to comply. They reluctantly did so, followed by the release of the Americans.

Despite the president's tough public stand against terror, his administration actually wavered a great deal in its handling of the problem. During his first week in office, the new president proclaimed "let terrorists be aware that . . . our policy will be one of swift and effective retribution." Secretary of State Alexander Haig equated terrorism with the Soviet threat as one of the two main dangers facing America. Shortly after sanctioning the TWA deal, Reagan told an assembly of the American Bar Association that "America will never make concessions to terrorists." He called Iran and Libya "outlaw states . . . run by the strangest collection of misfits, Looney Tunes, and squalid criminals since the advent of the Third Reich."

In practice, the Reagan administration often bent the rules. For example, in the mid-1980s, the Justice Department had a chance to seize in Greece Mohammed Rashid, a terrorist working for Iraq, believed responsible for many bombings of American, European, and Israeli targets. But by 1985–86 the United States was supplying high technology equipment to Iraq and assisting it in its war with Iran. The National Security Council, and particularly Lt. Colonel Oliver North, blocked the Justice Department so that nothing interfered with the new "special relationship" with Iraq.

By the same token, American officials sometimes defended or even abetted terrorist acts by groups Washington supported. For example, the CIA trained and equipped *contra* guerrillas in Nicaragua to attack economic targets and civilians linked even indirectly to the Sandinistas. In Beirut, William Casey probably authorized payment in March 1985 to Sunni Muslims who planned to blow up a Shi'ite cleric. The targeted sheik survived, although eighty Lebanese civilians were killed by the car bomb intended for him.

Also, as Reagan's friends knew, the plight of the seven American hostages held in Lebanon, and their families' grief, moved him deeply. The president tended to confuse human interest with the national interest, substituting the immediate emotional rewards of freeing hostages for the long-term strategy of removing the causes—and rewards—of terrorism.

Reagan felt terrible anguish when the families of the seven Americans held hostage in Lebanon pleaded with him to negotiate their release. The circumstance differed greatly from the problem confronting Jimmy Carter. With the exception of hostage William Buckley, a CIA agent, all those captive in Beirut were private citizens who had ignored State Department advice to stay out of Lebanon. Still, Reagan wanted everything possible done to win their freedom.

In July 1985 David Kimche, an Israeli official, introduced Iranian businessman Manucher Ghorbanifar to National Security Adviser Robert McFarlane. Ghorbanifar claimed to represent Iranian "moderates" who favored closer ties to the United States and the release of the Americans held in Beirut by pro-Iranian Lebanese. Ghorbanifar asked that Reagan show his "good faith" by selling anti-tank missiles to his Iranian friends. They would use these weapons in the war against Iraq, lobby to free the American hostages, and, upon Ayatollah Khomeini's "imminent" death (an event that occurred four years later) move to improve ties with Washington.

Israeli involvement in facilitating contacts between the Reagan administration and the so-called Iranian moderates provides another, if indirect, clue about possible earlier Reagan involvement with Iran. As far back as the fall of 1980, during the presidential campaign, Israel had sold to Iran American-licensed military equipment. Admiral Stansfield Turner, President Carter's CIA director, later suggested this might have been part of the effort by Reagan's campaign aides to induce the Iranians not to release the hostages before the November election. Following Reagan's election and inauguration, Israel, with U.S. knowledge, increased its weapons shipments to Iran, despite the public effort of the American government to embargo arms sales during 1981 and 1982.

Despite all the uncertainties, the idea appealed to National Security Adviser Robert McFarlane. For some time he had urged the president to improve relations with Iran as a way of limiting Soviet influence, containing Iraq, and expanding the U.S. role in the Persian Gulf. Even though most State and Defense Department experts disparaged this idea and saw few signs that any moderates could be found in Iran, McFarlane envisioned himself playing the same role as Henry Kissinger when he had opened ties to China under Nixon. The National Security Adviser broached the idea to Reagan on July 13, 1985, as the president entered the hospital for removal of a cancerous growth. Reagan encouraged the plan ("Gee, that sounds pretty good," McFarlane remembered him as saying), stressing the point in his presidential diary that contacts with Iran might help get "our seven kidnap victims back." He said nothing about building a new "strategic relationship" with Iran.

Pursuing the initiative depended on getting the Israelis to act as middlemen (technically, they would sell the weapons and the Pentagon would replenish their stockpile, thus skirting the legal prohibition against U.S. weapons sales to Iran) and on judging the reliability of the Iranian contact. The Israelis insisted that Reagan personally authorize arms sales before they acted. As for Ghorbanifar, those who knew him well realized that he maintained links with many factions in the Middle East. Despite a CIA report that dismissed him as a "fabricator and nuisance," McFarlane judged him reliable.

On August 6, McFarlane briefed Reagan, Vice President Bush, Secretary of State Shultz, and Secretary of Defense Weinberger on his proposal to sell Iran, via Israel, 100 TOW anti-tank missiles in order to secure the release of four hostages. Shultz and Weinberger criticized this as a "very bad idea." Bush remained silent. Reagan asked few questions and pondered the request for a few days before deciding.

He then telephoned McFarlane and gave his verbal approval. (In January 1987, Reagan admitted this sequence of events to investigators, then, when aides told him it made him culpable, he changed his testimony to say he could not remember if he had authorized McFarlane's action in advance.) On August 20, on American instructions, the Israelis shipped about 100 TOWs to Iran. To override the restriction on selling weapons to Iran the president would have had to sign a formal waiver and notify Congress. Reagan refused to do either. Instead, he ordered replacement missiles shipped to Israel.

The deliveries went smoothly but no hostages were freed. Instead, Ghorbanifar reported that the Iranians wanted 400 more missiles in exchange for one hostage. McFarlane, who now brought in Oliver North to help him, demanded the release of the CIA's William Buckley who, in fact, had already been killed by his captors. On September 14, an Israeli plane delivered about 400 TOWs to Iran and on the next day Reverend Benjamin Weir was set free in Beirut. North wrote the welcome home statement for the president. North shielded his operation by allowing Church of England envoy Terry Waite to take public credit for arranging hostage releases in 1985–86. Waite, who was himself kidnapped in Beirut in January 1987 and held for almost five years, seems to have known nothing about the arms sales. NSC staff member Howard Teicher called him an innocent "cover."

In November 1985, Ghorbanifar offered to broker the release of more hostages in return for 100 HAWK anti-aircraft missiles. McFarlane called this a straight "arms for hostages deal," and North wrote a memorandum saying "120 Hawks = five American citizens and guarantees that no more will be taken." Around this time, a few HAWKs were delivered to Iran from Israeli stocks, but they were obsolete models rejected by the Iranians.

By the beginning of December, McFarlane felt "burned out" and resigned his post. Reagan appointed his deputy, Admiral John Poindexter to replace him as National Security Adviser. Poindexter, a reclusive individual ill at ease with White House intrigue, relied even more heavily on Oliver North than had McFarlane. North proposed expanding arms sales to Iran by selling several thousand anti-tank and anti-aircraft missiles. The weapons would be delivered in stages, calibrated to release of the Beirut hostages. Unless sales were continued, North warned, vengeful Lebanese might kill the captive Americans.

Before proceeding, Poindexter had the president sign a retroactive "finding" early in December justifying the previous arms sales. The document, kept secret and later destroyed by Poindexter, described the weapons transfer as an arms for hostage deal. Again, little was said about forging a relationship with Iranian moderates.

Outside the president and the NSC staff, the operation had few advocates. Angered by the release of a single hostage, Secretary of State Shultz cautioned Reagan about falling victim to the extortion of "Iranian rug merchants." Defense Secretary Weinberger and even Chief of Staff Donald Regan, originally a supporter of the scheme, urged the president to "cut his losses." But Reagan remained adamant that the operation continue. This determination, despite the grave political risks and lack of results, former CIA director Turner speculates, might have resulted from Reagan's fear that if he broke off contact Iran would reveal his involvement in earlier arms deals, stretching back to the 1980 campaign.

North's "Neat Idea"

Because the price charged Iran for the missiles and spare parts exceeded their replacement cost, the initial sale, via Israel, had produced a profit of a few hundred thousand dollars. Oliver North spent it on behalf of the *contras*. He joked that the Ayatollah had made a *"contra*bution." This, the colonel later explained, inspired him to "use the Ayatollah Khomeini's money to support the Nicaraguan freedom fighters." He described it as a "neat idea." North believed it legal to use arms sales, profits to aid the *contras* since the Boland Amendment only barred spending money actually appropriated by Congress.

The colonel had a poor knowledge of the law. His plan relied on selling government property (missiles) at a profit. Federal statutes required that such profits be returned to the Treasury and also barred the executive branch from spending any funds that Congress had not appropriated. President Reagan later insisted he had "never heard a whisper about funds being channeled from the Iranian arms shipments to the *contras*" and "would not have approved it if anyone suggested it to me."

In January 1987, a few months after the scandal broke, the president acknowledged that an illegal deal might have occurred without his knowledge. But by the time he left office two years later, Reagan claimed that "no hard proof" existed of any diversion of funds whatsoever. This remarkable assertion contradicted the president's own investigation (the Tower Commission, discussed below), sworn testimony before Congress, and even the confessions of the principal culprits—Robert McFarlane, John Poindexter, and Oliver North. At his criminal trial in 1990, Admiral Poindexter testified that Reagan not only knew about but encouraged the diversion, an assertion that the president consistently denied. North, too, later claimed that President Reagan knew of and approved of the sale of arms to Iran and the diversion of profits to the *contras*.

In February 1986 North arranged the sale to Iran of 1,000 TOW missiles. This netted a profit of between $6 and $10 million for Secord to use for purchasing weapons for the *contras*. But, again, the deal yielded no liberated hostages. After eight months of contacts and several arms shipments from both American and Israeli stockpiles, the NSC operation had freed one American.

In the spring of 1986, the Iranians demanded more weapons and better intelligence data on Iraq before making more deals. By this time North's concern for the hostages had to compete with his need to continue the arms sales in any case to earn profits for the Nicaraguan guerrillas. Robert McFarlane (now retired from the NSC but still involved in the operation) still believed the contacts would yield strategic benefits as well as freedom for the Beirut captives.

During May the two men proposed a daring venture to free all the remaining captives with one large, overpriced, arms shipment. After securing the president's blessing on May 25, 1986 (this, just a month after Reagan had ordered the Air Force to bomb Libya in retaliation for Col. Qaddafi's sponsorship of terrorism), Mc-Farlane and North using pseudonyms, flew to the Iranian capital carrying a small load of missile parts, a gift-wrapped brace of .357 pistols, a Bible, a birthday cake decorated with a brass key for Ghorbanifar's mother, and suicide pills—for use should they be taken captive.

McFarlane offered to dispatch a plane loaded with weapons to Teheran in return for the freedom of all the Americans held in Beirut. The Iranians stalled, insisting the arms come first. They also demanded that Washington arrange the release of several Shi'ite terrorists, known as the Dawa prisoners, jailed in Kuwait for murder. Anxious to keep the profitable arms deal in play, North urged McFarlane to consider these terms. McFarlane, however, broke off negotiations and after four days the delegation left Iran empty-handed.

The next month, on June 25, 1986, Congress bowed to administration pressure and voted to resume aid to the *contras*. This would provide the CIA and NSC with legal funds for use against the Sandinistas. However, Congress stipulated the money would not become available until October, creating a four-month cash flow bottleneck. North set to work on another arms deal, hoping to raise money and secure the release of a hostage in time for the July 4 extravaganza the president would host at the re-opening of the Statue of Liberty. The NSC staffer imagined the sensation that would ensue if, on live TV, Reagan welcomed back a hostage at the Statue. Ghorbanifar shared this sense of theater, informing his Iranian contacts "we would exploit it and benefit from it a great deal; we could get the Americans to accept many of our demands." But the release failed to come off in time. Later that month, however, the Iranians rekindled American interest by securing the freedom of hostage Father Lawrence Jenco. North then got Poindexter and Reagan to approve an August shipment of HAWK-missile components to Iran.

By then the Iranians had learned that the Americans were overcharging them for the missiles. Meanwhile, North finally realized that Ghorbanifar was playing both sides of the street. Incredibly, instead of abandoning the operation, and totally ignoring the fact that additional Americans had just been kidnapped in Beirut, North received approval from President Reagan and John Poindexter to initiate a new contact with Iran, via a young man named Ali Hashemi Bahremani, nephew of Ali Akbar Hashemi Rafsanjani, the speaker of the Iranian parliament. North met with Bahremani both in Washington and Frankfurt, Germany, during September and October 1986, even escorting the Iranian on a midnight tour of the White House. He gave Bahremani a Bible inscribed by the president, and promised new arms sales and help freeing the Dawa terrorists jailed in Kuwait if some (not all) of the Americans held in Beirut were freed before the November 4 congressional election. At one meeting, North claimed he had already cleared the way by meeting with the "Kuwaiti foreign minister secretly, in my spare time between blowing up Nicaragua."

On American instructions, Israel shipped 500 TOW anti-tank missiles to Iran at the end of October. North informed the White House they should prepare to announce a hostage release "before CNN knows it has happened." Hostage David Jacobsen was set free in Beirut on November 2, although the event failed to attract the attention North expected and did little to sway voters who restored a Democratic majority to the Senate. In fact, instead of "scooping CNN," the Reagan administration faced a grave crisis.

The Scandal Surfaces

The "neat idea" began to unravel on October 5, 1986, just two weeks before legal aid to the *contras* could resume, when Sandinista gunners shot down a cargo plane ferrying weapons purchased by General Secord for delivery to the guerrillas. One crew member, Eugene Hasenfus, survived the crash and confessed to his Sandinista interrogators that he was part of a secret American government-aid program. Although he knew only a few details,

Hasenfus provided enough information eventually to reveal critical parts of the arms supply network.

During a dramatic press conference in Managua on October 9, 1986, a bruised and bandaged Hassenfus described his final mission. He had already flown ten military supply flights on behalf of the *contras,* he explained, all under the direction of CIA employees. He named Max Gomez, the code name of CIA official Felix Rodriguez, as his chief contact. These revelations led top agency officials such as Claire George and Alan Fiers to concoct false testimony denying all Hassenfus's assertions, when Central American task force director Fiers appeared shortly afterward before the Senate Intelligence Committee. Speaking after the shootdown, William Casey told North what he must do with the *contra*-aid program: "shut it down and clean it up" and be prepared to take the blame.

On November 3, a day before Americans went to the polls, *Al Shiraa,* an obscure Lebanese magazine, printed a slightly garbled account of the arms for hostages deal. Within hours, top Iranian officials confirmed the story, adding that the so-called moderates were actually loyal agents of the Ayatollah Khomeini bilking the western infidels. As Americans voted on November 4, the media made only passing reference to the explosive revelations coming from the Middle East. But the story became a sensation hours after the polls closed.

Even as American journalists began uncovering the tangled threads of the arms for hostage deals, administration officials denied most knowledge of it. On November 8, Oliver North even met again with an Iranian representative to discuss another trade. However, Iran made it clear that no more Americans would be set free until the Shi'ite terrorists in Kuwait were released. The president, North, and Poindexter still believed they could contain or even profit from the scandal by selectively releasing information. "We have a damn good story to tell when we are ready," Poindexter assured his colleagues. He encouraged Reagan to say nothing, predicting the fuss would soon blow over.

As part of a cover-up, North, Poindexter, CIA director Casey, and other top intelligence officials released misleading information and false chronologies to Congress and the press between November 10 and November 21. Among other deceptions, they tried to put the blame on Secretary of State Shultz, who had opposed the scheme, claimed they had only authorized the sale to Iran of "oil drilling equipment," and suggested Israel had masterminded the whole operation.

President Reagan spoke publicly on the subject on November 13, comparing the initiative to Nixon's historic opening to China in 1971. He blamed the media for hyping the story and insisted his administration had done nothing more than transfer "small amounts of defensive weapons and spare parts" to Iran. Reagan repeated the cover story that he did so to bolster the power of moderate elements, speed an end to the Iran-Iraq war, and encourage the release of hostages in Beirut, "We did not—repeat did not—trade weapons or anything else for hostages nor will we." None of these assertions was accurate.

Meanwhile, the president asked Attorney General Edwin Meese to conduct an inquiry into the affair. Meese moved slowly, took no notes of what anyone told him, and made so little effort to safeguard evidence that North and his staff had several days to destroy incriminating materials. Poindexter, North and NSC secretary Fawn Hall held what they later called a "shredding party" to destroy some 5,000 pages of documents. When the shredding machine jammed, Hall smuggled sensitive papers out of the NSC office in her boots and underwear. Some of this activity continued even while Meese's staff was present in the NSC offices. Unhappily for the conspirators, enough material survived on back-up tapes on the NSC master computer to raise grave concerns about the competence and truthfulness of the Reagan administration.

On November 22, the Attorney General learned that a member of his staff found a portion of a document dated April 4, 1986, in North's files that explicitly linked the arms sales to the diversion of between $10 million and $20 million to the *contras*. The next day Meese asked North to explain the meaning of this and then incredibly allowed him continued access to NSC files—and the paper shredder—for several more hours before sealing them. The Attorney General informed the president of the discovery on November 24 and the next day they made it public.

Up to the time on November 25 when Meese and Reagan held a news conference revealing evidence of the diversion, some of the president's aides still believed they could contain the damage if the

Israeli government agreed to take the blame for initiating the arms sales. But when Israel publicly refused to take the rap, Reagan decided to purge the NSC staff. On November 25 he announced Poindexter's "resignation" and North's firing. A few hours before he had telephoned Oliver North, called him a "national hero" whose "work will make a great movie someday," then explained he was being fired. If, as the president claimed, he was in the dark about the whole affair, it seems curious that at no time did he bother to ask either man what they had or had not done in his name.

As the Iran-Contra scandal unfolded during the last weeks of 1986, the president stuck to his claim that he knew nothing about any arms for hostage deal or diversion of profits to fund the *contras*. Pollsters found that only about one American in seven believed him. By December 2, Reagan's overall approval rating plummeted from 67% to 46%, the sharpest one-month drop in a president's public opinion rating ever recorded by the Gallup Organization.

Iran-Contra Hearings

Shortly after Attorney General Meese revealed that the NSC staff had sold arms to the Ayatollah and diverted profits to the *contras,* the president named a special review panel chaired by former Texas Senator John Tower and including former Secretary of State Edmund Muskie and former National Security Adviser Brent Scowcroft. The so-called Tower Commission was one of three official bodies investigating what became known as the Iran-Contra affair. A joint congressional committee and a special prosecutor, Lawrence Walsh, also probed the events.

The Tower Commission took testimony and reviewed documents during January 1987. The president's presentations proved rambling and contradictory. He avoided responding to some critical questions and answered others by citing irrelevant anecdotes. In the end, he claimed to be unable to remember whether or not he had authorized arms sales to Iran. The other principals either refused to testify or provided misleading information.

The report released by the Tower board on February 26, 1987, presented the first coherent account of the episode. As Reagan hoped, it exonerated him from charges of law breaking. The report described Reagan as remote, disengaged, uninformed, and easily manipulated by aides. The president's action "ran directly counter" to his promise to deal harshly with terrorism, thereby undermining the nation's prestige and reputation. Yet, the report stressed, nothing linked Reagan directly to illegal acts or the diversion of the profits. Rather, due to his lax "management style," zealous subordinates probably "duped" him. This conclusion portrayed the president as a well-intentioned, laid-back fellow not always sure of the facts. At worst a fool, but not a knave.

The president effectively blunted even this rap on the knuckles by appearing on television on March 4 to accept contritely the findings of the Tower report—while denying any real responsibility. Reagan had neither read the report nor played much of a role in drafting his apology. Still, he told the viewing public that even if the facts suggested he agreed to pay ransom to kidnappers, in his "heart" he never meant to trade arms for hostages. A day after the president's speech, his approval rating shot up ten points. He deflected some more of the blame by firing Chief of Staff Donald Regan following the release of the Tower report. Although Regan had been only a bit player in the scandal, the president appeared to be cleaning house.

The joint Senate-House investigation, under the chairmenship of Senator Daniel Inouye, Democrat of Hawaii, and Representative Lee Hamilton, Democrat of Indiana, proved cumbersome and ineffective. Although scrupulously fair, Inouye and Hamilton imposed a number of awkward rules on the inquiry. In order to prevent the case from dragging on into the 1988 presidential race, they set an arbitrary termination date of October 1987 for the hearings. The committee decided against calling either Reagan or Vice President Bush to testify. To assure the timely testimony of Oliver North and some other participants, the committee agreed to grant them immunity from criminal prosecution for anything they said at the hearings. This eventually made it nearly impossible to prosecute North in court for his activities.

The lawyers for the joint committee focused on the money trail, trying to discover how the profits of the arms sales were diverted to the *contras,* who authorized the policy, and who profited from it. Despite promises of cooperation, the Reagan administration actually blocked the release of many vital documents. The CIA either refused to permit its key operatives to testify about their role in the affair or ordered them to falsify testimony and deny any knowledge of either the arms sales to Iran or diversion of funds to supply the *contras*. As a result, it became impossible to reach definitive conclusions within the alloted time limit.

Much of the testimony during the summer of 1987 focused on the activities of Oliver North, whom one participant described as "the world's most powerful lieutenant colonel." The telegenic North dominated the hearings through his vigorous defense of his own actions and his president. He chided Congress for ignoring the Sandinista threat and declared that he and Reagan had a moral responsibility to protect national security in spite of prohibitions imposed by Congress or the law.

On camera, North preened and boasted, swelled up his breast to fill his medal-bedecked uniform. He described himself as totally loyal to his superiors, prepared "to take a spear in the chest" to protect them. In reality, North's testimony proved both self-serving and damaging to Reagan. He suggested that all his superiors, including the president, knew about and sanctioned his illegal activities. (North stressed this point in his memoirs, published in 1991, declaring "President Reagan knew everything.")

The impression television viewers came away with, however, was of a brassy, brave, and selfless patriot. He might have cut some corners, but always out of duty. Newspapers spoke of "Olliemania," a groundswell of support for the flamboyant officer. His flagwaving narrative obscured the legal and moral squalor of the operation—including the interesting fact that the North–Secord–Hakim arms supply network siphoned off for their own use a major part of the money supposed to go to the *contras*. The guerrillas may have received as little as 20 cents on the dollar from the various sources tapped by North.

Former National Security Adviser Admiral John Poindexter protected the president more directly by denying that Reagan knew of or authorized the diversion of funds. He insisted that "the buck stops with me." CIA director William Casey, ill with a fatal brain tumor, never testified and took his secrets to the grave. Confronted by uncooperative and frequently dishonest witnesses, lack

Lt. Colonel Oliver North testifies before Congress in 1987. *Courtesy AP/Wide World Photos.*

of access to critical documents, and pressure to wrap up the inquiry quickly, Congress reached no real verdict.

In March 1988 Special Prosecutor Lawrence Walsh indicted North, Poindexter, Channel, Secord, Hakim, and others involved in the scandal.[1] Eventually, all were convicted or pled guilty to charges of perjury, misusing government funds, and other infractions. (A later federal appeals court ruling overturned the convictions of North and Poindexter on the grounds that immunized testimony before Congress made it nearly impossible for prosecutors, witnesses, and a jury not to have been influenced by that testimony. The special prosecutor had to drop all charges against North and Poindexter in late 1991.) At his trial in 1990, Admiral Poindexter repudiated his previous testimony before Congress and declared that the president knew all the details of the Iran-Contra operation and had ordered him to break the law and destroy documents. Reagan, in a videotaped interrogation during the Poindexter trial, appeared painfully confused and unable to remember most names, dates, or events concerned with the scandal. He denied any knowledge of his subordinates' misdeeds.

Ultimately, Congress, the Tower Commission, and the special prosecutor hardly laid a glove on Reagan. Members of the House and Senate hesitated to accept evidence linking him directly to illegal acts. They feared popular retribution if Congress were blamed for bringing down another chief executive, especially one who had only one more year to serve and retained an affectionate hold on most Americans. For its part, the public forgave Reagan's ignorance and mismanagement, so long as nothing surfaced that linked him directly to law breaking.

Members of Congress also misjudged the public's ire about Iran-Contra. The diversion of funds to the *contras*, which became the centerpiece of the investigation, did not particularly disturb most

---

[1] In September 1991 Alan Fiers pled guilty to lying about his knowledge of CIA involvement in Iran-Contra. On the basis of his testimony, Special Counsel Walsh indicted Claire George, the CIA's former director of Clandestine Operations. In October Elliott Abrams, former Assistant Secretary of State, pled guilty to lying to Congress about his knowledge of illegal efforts to arm the *contras*. In November 1991 Walsh charged Duane R. Clarridge with lying to Congress when he denied knowledge of a 1985 arms shipment to Iran.

Americans. People felt far more strongly about dealing with the hated Ayatollah Khomeini and the hypocrisy of denouncing terrorism while negotiating with kidnappers, but the hearings did not concentrate on this aspect of law breaking. Nor did the investigation highlight the larger pattern of midconduct in administration foreign policy.

Summit Politics

Something extraneous to the affair also salvaged Reagan's presidency. By the summer of 1987, rapidly improving relations with the Soviet Union distracted attention from the shabby Iran-Contra episode. The Democrats, who now controlled Congress, favored a relaxation of Cold War tensions. With Reagan willing to negotiate with the Soviets, they had a strong incentive to mute criticism of his other lapses.

Until 1985, Reagan had refused to meet with any Soviet leader. After that year, he spent more time with his Kremlin counterpart than any previous president. Reagan conferred with Mikhail Gorbachev in Geneva in November 1985, Reykjavik, Iceland, in October 1986, Washington in December 1987, Moscow in June 1988, and New York in December 1988. Their relationship evolved because of changes in both countries.

Mikhail Gorbachev became General Secretary of the Soviet Communist Party in March 1985, succeeding three consecutive invalids. Unusually young for a Soviet leader at age 54, he was also well educated, travelled, and undogmatic. After taking power, he blamed his three predecessors for presiding over a twenty-year "period of stagnation." Gorbachev acknowledged publicly that the Soviet Union had fallen far behind the economic and technological progress of most western and many Asian nations. Soviet industry produced insufficient and shoddy goods. The defense sector absorbed a prohibitive amount of capital and resources. The old methods of central planning and authoritarian control yielded diminishing returns.

Gorbachev proclaimed new policies of *perestroika* (social and economic restructuring) and *glasnost* (openness and democracy), reforms that by 1991 transformed the fundamental existence of the Soviet Union and communism. The Soviet leadership began permitting freer elections and encouraged moves toward a market economy. Wrenching the U.S.S.R. out of its torpor, Gorbachev concluded, required cooperation with the capitalist community. He courted European leaders and insisted that he represented a new type of communism. Britain's conservative prime minister and close Reagan friend, Margaret Thatcher, described Gorbachev as "charming" and someone with whom the West could do business.

President Reagan resisted Gorbachev's blandishments longer than most western leaders. By most accounts, including her own, Nancy Reagan played an important role in arranging a summit conference. She believed that a relaxation of cold war tension would solidify her husband's accomplishments. In a "dangerous world," she later remarked, it was "ridiculous for the two heavily armed superpowers to be sitting there and not talking to each other." Mrs. Reagan found support for this view from her astrologer, Joan Quigley.

Quigley later revealed that before the president agreed to meet Gorbachev in Geneva, Nancy Reagan asked her to interpret Gorbachev's Zodiac. The astrologer informed the First Lady that Gorbachev's "Aquarian planet is in such harmony with Ronnie's . . . they'll share a vision." The president's "evil empire attitude" would "have to go." In any event, Nancy Reagan explained, that while she and Quigley did "push Ronnie a little," he "would never have met Gorbachev if he hadn't wanted to."

Nevertheless, the first summit, at Geneva in November 1985, went only moderately well. The two leaders' wives certainly shared no vision and got into a spat. "Who does this dame think she is?," Nancy complained when Raisa tried to dominate a photo session. The two leaders also sparred. Reagan criticized the Soviet Union for violating the SALT and ABM treaties, denounced its record on human rights, and repeated his determination to build SDI. Gorbachev disputed these assertions and charged that any Star Wars deployment would violate the anti-missile treaty.

The mood improved at a dinner when the subject turned toward film. The president expressed irritation at a remark by a Soviet official who described him as a star of "grade B movies." They "weren't all B movies," Reagan told Gorbachev. The Soviet leader replied that "the one I liked was the young man without legs." He referred, of course, to Reagan's favorite film, *King's Row*. Both Raisa and Mikhail Gorbachev turned out to be movie buffs and, one participant reported, sat "spellbound . . . by every detail" the president told them about Hollywood. They were "very pleased," Chief of Staff Donald Regan recalled, "to be in the company of somebody who had known Jimmy Stewart, John Wayne and Humphrey Bogart."

Perhaps because of this rapport, Reagan confided to Gorbachev his belief that if Earth were invaded by hostile aliens, the two superpowers would surely cooperate. Although this assertion stunned the Soviet leader (Reagan frequently discussed alien visitations with his staff), the president's biographer, Lou Cannon, suggests this was merely Reagan's way of stating that the survival of humanity justified dealing with the "lesser evil" of the Soviet Union.

The Geneva summit improved "atmospherics" but did not end the rivalry of the two superpowers. Reagan and Gorbachev met a second time at Reykjavik, Iceland, in October 1986. For reasons that remain unclear, the president proposed this conference with little preparation. Some observers speculated he sought to achieve some sort of breakthrough on the eve of the November 4, 1986, mid-term election.

Early on, Gorbachev seized the initiative. He knew Reagan favored the elimination, not just limitation, of nuclear weapons. The Soviet leader proposed a mutual 50% cut in the number of long-range ballistic missiles while pledging to work for their eventual elimination. In return, however, the anti-missile treaty must be strictly observed for ten more years, confining SDI research to the laboratory. The Soviets continued to fear Star Wars technology even though most American scientists doubted the missile shield would ever work. Only Reagan and the men in the Kremlin, some cynics quipped, took the plan seriously.

During a recess, George Shultz and Defense Department hard-liner Richard Perle, urged Reagan to make a bold counteroffer. The president now proposed to eliminate *all* American (and possibly British and French, as well) ballistic missiles over a ten-year period. But at the end of the process, the United States would be free to deploy SDI as insurance against cheating, accidents, or threats from a third country. Perle, an opponent of arms control, probably expected Gorbachev to reject this since, if accepted, it would leave the Americans with a big advantage in strategic bombers and cruise missiles.

But Gorbachev was not to be outdone. He now suggested eliminating all of the world's nuclear weapons, not just their delivery systems. This would neutralize the advantage Perle hoped for. Reagan must, however, agree not to deploy the yet-to-be built SDI. The president was intrigued by this idea until, in his words, Gorbachev "threw us a curve" by saying "all depends, of course, on your giving up SDI." Reagan shouted that SDI was not a "bargaining chip" and ended the summit.

The president's advisers were relieved that no agreement had been reached. The American leader had no authority to eliminate British and French weapons. Since Reagan had long complained that Moscow enjoyed a substantial conventional military advantage, it seemed strange for him to offer to surrender the West's nuclear deterrent without a large carefully monitored reduction in Soviet conventional forces. National Security Adviser Poindexter told Reagan "we've got to clear up this business about you agreeing to get rid of all nuclear weapons." Reagan replied, "But John, I did agree to that." "No," Poindexter argued, "you couldn't have." The president persisted. "I was there, and I did." Frustrated by Reagan's loose talk, Chief of Staff Donald Regan told a reporter after the summit that "some of us are like a shovel brigade that follows a parade down Main Street cleaning up."

Toward the End of the Cold War

It would have been difficult to predict that a major thaw in the Cold War would emerge from such discussions. Yet, during 1987, in the wake of the Iran-Contra scandal, President Reagan replaced several of his hardline, anti-Soviet advisers. Former Senator Howard Baker took over as chief of staff after Donald Regan's firing in February. The death of William Casey led to the appointment of FBI Director William Webster to head the CIA. Poindexter's firing cleared the way for Frank Carlucci to head the National Security Council. Caspar Weinberger's resignation a few months later resulted in Carlucci's promotion to Defense Secretary. Lt. Gen. Colin Powell succeeded Carlucci as National Security Adviser.

This new team, more moderate and less driven by reflexive anti-communism, proved far more receptive to the goals of arms control and detente with the Soviet Union. They found a strong ally in Nancy Reagan. A fierce defender of her husband's image, she hoped a breakthrough with Gorbachev, not the squalid Iran-Contra mess, would become the president's foreign policy legacy.

In the autumn of 1987, Soviet and American negotiators agreed on a treaty to remove all intermediate-range nuclear-tipped missiles (INF) from Europe. Although these missiles formed only a tiny portion of the total nuclear arsenal, the pact represented the first time the two superpowers had agreed to destroy a whole category of weapons. Gorbachev surprised everyone by accepting a long-standing American demand for mutual on-site inspection to assure compliance.

The Soviets made most of the concessions, dropping their demand that an INF treaty be linked to limits on long-range missiles and SDI. Gorbachev had probably concluded that Star Wars would not be built in the foreseeable future. Reagan argued that his massive defense buildup and tough approach brought the Russians around. He also asserted he knew the pressure would work because in 1986 he learned the Soviets faced a major economic crisis.

Reagan surely oversimplified. The grave problems in the Soviet economy began long before 1986. What changed was Gorachev's willingness to acknowledge this publicly and his decision to stop bleeding the civilian economy to support armaments. He recognized that modernization required Western and Japanese help. Gorbachev's sense of international relations also differed from his predecessors. Since Stalin's time, if not before, Soviet and Russian leaders measured security by the degree to which Moscow dominated or intimidated neighbors and rivals. Gorbachev sought to enhance Soviet security through cooperation with neighboring states and other world powers. As early as 1947, diplomat George Kennan predicted that a long-term policy of containment of Soviet power would eventually achieve just this result. It took forty years, but Kennan, as much as Reagan, deserves credit for the achievement. As many observers also noted, the president was on shaky ground when he boasted that the arms buildup had broken the Soviet economy since its effects in the United States were nearly as severe.

Mikhail Gorbachev visited Washington in December 1987 to sign the INF treaty. Undaunted by his guest's charm, the president

Reagan and Soviet President Mikhail Gorbachev sign the INF Treaty. *Courtesy U.S. National Archives.*

quipped, "I don't resent his popularity. Good Lord, I co-starred with Errol Flynn once." This joculatory, apparently so easy and unforced, reaped immense popular appreciation for Reagan.

Gorbachev showed a flair for generating attention by hosting a party for American luminaries such as Paul Newman, Yoko Ono, and Henry Kissinger. He charmed members of Congress. Pedestrians in Washington were thrilled when the Soviet leader jumped out of his limousine and grabbed their hands. "I just want to say hello to you," he gushed. The only criticism came from a small core of Reagan's most conservative backers. Angered at his sudden friendliness with Moscow, one called the president a "useful idiot" of the communist conspiracy.

Aside from the INF treaty, the two Cold War rivals reached few substantive agreements during the remainder of Reagan's term. Both leaders, however, got a boost in their ratings from improved relations and agreed to meet in Moscow in June 1988. In a sense, the thaw in the Cold War insulated Reagan and Gorbachev from a host of domestic problems.

The mere fact of Reagan's appearance in Moscow significantly blunted the edges of the Cold War. Asked if he still considered the Soviets the "focus of evil in the modern world," he answered, "They've changed." The president actually embraced Gorbachev at Lenin's tomb. During the Moscow meeting, George Shultz was impressed that Gorbachev seemed determined to match Reagan "joke for joke." Ever attuned to symbolism, the president reported that he "knew the world was changing" when he stood at attention beside the Soviet leader at the Bolshoi Ballet and a Soviet orchestra played "The Star-Spangled Banner." Although the two superpowers still had more than 30,000 nuclear weapons aimed at each other, in the new spirit of the time, few people worried.

During 1988, the Soviets withdrew their troops from Afghanistan and supported efforts to end civil conflicts in Ethiopia, Angola, and Southeast Asia. The dormant United Nations re-emerged as a key forum for mediating these disputes. Reagan met Gorbachev again, in December in New York, where the Soviet leader announced plans to reduce conventional forces. Increasingly attuned to public relations, Gorbachev invited Reagan and President-elect George Bush to pose for pictures with him in front of the Statue of Liberty. As it became fashionable to proclaim the end of the Cold War, even the wives of the two leaders made peace. The *New York Times* headlined: "Another Obstacle Falls: Nancy Reagan and Raisa Gorbachev get Chummy."

Conclusion

Against all odds, the most assertive anti-communist president since the Second World War achieved a foreign policy goal that had eluded his predecessors. Because of breakthroughs in arms control, new cooperation in settling Third World disputes, and an overall relaxation in tensions, the two superpowers charted a radically altered course. Inside the Soviet Union, the political and economic reforms initiated by Mikhail Gorbachev presaged the end of Soviet domination of Eastern Europe that began the year after Reagan left office. Probably nothing more graphically symbolized the waning of the Cold War and the bankruptcy of communism than the demolition of the Berlin Wall in 1989, something Reagan had called for

Reagan speaking at Moscow State University, beneath bust of Lenin.
Courtesy U.S. National Archives.

two years earlier. By the end of 1991, the Soviet Union, Reagan's "Evil Empire," had ceased to exist as a nation.

These dramatic events occurred during Reagan's presidency and naturally he and his supporters take credit for them. As early as June 1982, Reagan recalled, he had told the British parliament that the Soviet Union faced a "revolutionary crisis." The Communist giant ran against the tide of human history, he declared, and a "global campaign of freedom" would soon prevail. But, in a sense, it was diplomat and Cold War architect George Kennan's prediction of 1947 that had finally come to pass: over the long run containment had forced the Soviet Union to change its ways.

Reagan's policy of "peace through strength" had less to do with the upheaval in the Soviet empire than he realized. The great arms buildup of his presidency added to overkill capacity but did not fundamentally alter the strategic balance. On the other hand, the legacy of immense budget deficits partly caused by the arms race weakened America's capacity to compete with the rising economic giants of Europe and Asia. In both Central America and the Middle East, the United States failed to create any degree of peace or stability. The Iran-Contra scandal showed the degree to which foreign affairs could go wrong under a president who cared little about detail or the law.

Nevertheless, Ronald Reagan demonstrated a capacity to respond to Soviet overtures creatively, whether or not he brought them about or fully comprehended them. He left to his successor, George Bush, the complex job of charting a path in the era of what was already being called the "new world order."

Conclusion

ACCEPTING THE Republican nomination for the presidency on August 15, 1980, Ronald Reagan spoke passionately about the "Divine Providence" that made America an "island of freedom." Convention delegates nodded with approval when he asked them to launch his campaign with a silent prayer especially for those fleeing oppression. The words evoked deep ideals in this and later audiences. Nearly nine years later, in his January 1989 Farewell Address to the American people, he asserted, "I was not a great communicator but I communicated great things." The "Reagan Revolution," he added, "always seemed more like The Great Rediscovery, a rediscovery of our values and our common sense."

The president's self-congratulatory assessment of his administration ("We meant to change a nation, and instead, we changed a world. . . . All in all, not bad, not bad at all.") deftly avoided any hint of the economic, social, and environmental problems or administrative scandals he bequeathed to his successor. He spoke of the new friendship with Moscow, not of the criminal foolishness surrounding Iran-Contra. Reagan retired with a public approval rating of 70%, higher than any president since Franklin Roosevelt. Friend and foe alike paid special homage to his ability to connect emotionally to the American people, to convince many of them that they were heroes in control of their own destiny.

As president, Reagan achieved many of the symbolic goals he

had pledged to strive for. The United States stood "tall" abroad, by 1989 the only true military superpower left in the world. It was easy to conclude that his policy of confronting the Soviet Union had broken the aggressive spirit of the Communist system and helped bring forth the new leadership that carried out such radical changes in Soviet foreign and domestic policies. As he promised, federal income tax rates had decreased, even if rising levies for Social Security and state taxes meant most Americans paid as much each year as before. Reagan's tax and defense policies also contributed to the swelling of the federal debt, something he had promised to curtail.

Neither Congress nor most Americans, according to polling data, favored the conservative social agenda promoted since 1981. Efforts to amend the Constitution to ban abortion, permit prayer in public school, and mandate a balanced budget had languished. Reagan achieved greater success with the appointment of conservative judges, to lower federal courts and the Supreme Court, who influenced policies on civil rights and liberties. Despite his criticism of judicial activists, the Reagan judiciary is likely to play a major role in redefining American life during the next generation.

The administration's approach to a variety of social problems, such as teenage pregnancy, drug abuse, and AIDS remained essentially negative. Teenagers were urged to remain chaste, ghetto youth to "just say no to drugs," and everyone cautioned to be monogamous and heterosexual to avoid disease. The result, not surprisingly, was a surge in the teenage pregnancy rate, a drug scourge among poor and minority youth, and the rapid spread of AIDS. Meanwhile, the prison inmate population doubled and the homeless emerged as a national scandal. Although administration policies did not create these problems, the federal government did little to alleviate them.

A combination of anti-government, anti-regulatory philosophy and Reagan's gross lack of concern with public ethics contributed to several major scandals in his administration. The corruption in the Department of Housing and Urban Development, for example, allowed unscrupulous individuals to skim hundreds of millions, perhaps billions, of dollars from programs intended to help house poorer Americans. Even this paled before the scope of the savings and loan collapse, a disaster that might eventually cost taxpayers $500 billion.

Reagan persuaded many Americans that, in his words, "government is the problem," while assuring them that the United States remained a unique community of rugged individualists. His use of words and symbols evoked a powerful belief that a past that never was could not only be restored but would secure America's role as "number one" in the world.

Sophisticates chuckled when astrologer Joan Quigley revealed her role as informal adviser to Nancy and Ronald Reagan. Before the president agreed to hold his first summit with Gorbachev, as before other important decisions, Mrs. Reagan asked Quigley to assure her husband that the Soviet leader's star chart was in harmony with his own. One is tempted to dismiss out of hand this explanation of the end of the Cold War until it is remembered that Stanislav Shatalin, one of Gorbachev's leading economic advisers at the time, shared the Reagans' belief in astrology.

As George Bush campaigned against Michael Dukakis in 1988 to pick up the mantle of leadership from Ronald Reagan, the American electorate debated issues such as flag burning and the weekend furlough from state prison of rapist Willie Horton. Remarkably little was said about the dire state of the economy, the lack of an energy policy, or America's inability to compete in world markets. This trivialization of political discourse was another legacy of the Reagan years.

Reagan succeeded, as few actors or politicians have, in persuading Americans to suspend their disbelief. It was an era when saying something made it so, when, as in a daydream, anything seemed possible. Deficits did not exist, were someone else's fault, or did not matter; the poor caused their own plight or were impoverished because they received too much money from the government; the wealthy, on the other hand, had been abused by not being permitted to keep more of their income; the homeless preferred to sleep on steam grates while teenage mothers and young crack users were free to "just say no" or go to jail; terrorism was evil, unless selling weapons to terrorists might free hostages or provide funds for anti-communist guerrillas.

These comforting truths appealed to Reagan and many who served and admired him. But as the United States approaches a new century with its "new world order," they seem more like stage props and less like a set of principles to guide national policy.

Bibliography

Adelman, Kenneth, L. *The Great Universal Embrace, Arms Summitry—A Skeptic's Account.* New York: Simon and Schuster, 1989.

Anderson, Martin. *Revolution.* New York: Harcourt Brace Jovanovich, 1988.

Barrett, Laurence I. *Gambling with History, Ronald Reagan in the White House.* New York: Doubleday, 1983.

Bell, Terrel, H. *The Thirteenth Man: A Reagan Cabinet Memoir.* New York: The Free Press, 1988.

Birnbaum, Jeffrey H. and Alan S. Murray. *Showdown at Gucci Gulch: Lawmakers, Lobbyists, and the Unlikely Triumph of Tax Reform.* New York: Random House, 1987.

Blumenthal, Sidney. *Our Long National Daydream.* New York, 1988.

Boyer, Paul, ed. *Reagan as President.* Chicago: Ivan R. Dee, Publisher, 1990.

Bradlee, Ben, Jr. *Guts and Glory: The Rise and Fall of Oliver North.* New York: Donald I. Fine, Inc., 1988.

Bruck, Connie. *The Predator's Ball: The Junk Bond Raiders and the Man Who Staked Them.* New York: American Lawyer/Simon & Schuster, 1988.

Cannon, Lou. *Reagan.* New York: G. P. Putnam's Sons, 1982.

———. *President Reagan: The Role of a Lifetime.* New York: Simon & Schuster, 1991.

Carroll, Peter. *It Seemed Like Nothing Happened: The Tragedy and Promise of America in the 1970s.* New Brunswick, N.J.: Rutgers University Press, 1990.

Cockburn, Leslie. *Out of Control: The Story of the Reagan Administration's Secret War in Nicaragua, the Illegal Arms Pipeline, and the Contra Drug Connection.* New York: Atlantic Monthly Press, 1988.

Dallek, Robert. *Ronald Reagan: The Politics of Symbolism.* Cambridge, Mass.: Harvard University Press, 1984.

Davis, Patti, with Maureen Strange Foster. *Home Front.* New York: Crown, 1986.

Deaver, Michael K., with Mickey Herskowitz. *Behind the Scenes.* New York: William Morrow, 1987.

Dingess, John. *Our Man in Panama: How General Noriega Used the United States—and Made Millions in Drugs and Arms.* New York: Random House, 1990.

Draper, Theodore. *A Very Thin Line: The Iran-Contra Affairs.* New York: Hill & Wang/Farrar, Strauss, Giroux, 1991.

Dugger, Ronnie. *On Reagan, The Man and His Presidency.* New York: McGraw-Hill, 1983.

Eddy, Paul, with Hugo Sabogal, and Sara Walden. *The Cocaine Wars.* New York: W. W. Norton & Co., 1988.

Ehrenreich, Barbara. *Fear of Falling, The Inner Life of the Middle Class.* New York: Pantheon, 1989.

——. *The Worst Years of Our Lives: Irreverent Notes from a Decade of Greed.* New York: Pantheon, 1990.

Emerson, Steve. *Secret Warriors: Inside the Covert Military Operations of the Reagan Administration.* New York: G. P. Putnam's Sons, 1988.

Friedman, Benjamin. *Day of Reckoning: The Consequences of American Economic Policy Under Reagan and After.* New York: Random House, 1988.

Germond, Jack W. and Jules Witcover. *Wake Us When It's Over: Presidential Politics of 1984.* New York: Macmillan, 1985.

Greider, William. *The Education of David Stockman and Other Americans.* New York: A Signet Book, 1986.

Gutman, Roy. *Banana Diplomacy, The Making of American Policy in Nicaragua 1981–1987.* New York: Simon & Schuster, 1987.

Hadden, Jeffrey K., and Anson Shupe. *Televangelism: Power and Politics on God's Frontier.* New York: Henry Holt and Co., 1988.

Haig, Alexander M., Jr. *Caveat: Realism, Reagan, and Foreign Policy.* New York: Macmillan, 1984.

Hersh, Seymour. *The Target Is Destroyed: What Really Happened to Flight 007.* New York: Random House, 1987.

Hertsgaard, Mark. *On Bended Knee.* New York: Farrar, Strauss, Giroux, 1988.

Johnson, Haynes. *Sleepwalking Through History: America in the Reagan Years.* New York: W. W. Norton and Co., 1991.

Kempe, Frederick. *Divorcing the Dictator: America's Bungled Affair with Noriega.* New York: G. P. Putnam's Sons, 1990.

Ledeen, Michael A. *Perilous Statecraft: An Insider's Account of the Iran-Contra Affair.* New York: Charles Scribner's Sons, 1988.

Lekachman, Robert. *Greed Is Not Enough: Reaganomics.* New York: Pantheon, 1982.

Lewis, Michael. *Liar's Poker.* New York: W. W. Norton & Co., 1989.

Mayer, Jane, and Doyle McManus. *Landslide, The Unmaking of the President, 1984–1988.* Boston: Houghton Mifflin Co., 1988.

Mayer, Martin. *The Greatest Ever Bank Robbery, The Collapse of the Savings and Loan Industry.* New York: 1990.

Mills, Nicholas, ed. *Culture in an Age of Greed.* Chicago: Ivan R. Dee, 1990.

Moldea, Dan E. *Dark Victory: Ronald Reagan, MCA and the Mob.* New York: Viking Press, 1986.

Niskanen, William A. *Reaganomics: An Insider's Account of the Politics and the People.* New York: Oxford University Press, 1988.

Noonan, Peggy. *What I Saw at the Revolution: A Political Life in the Reagan Era.* New York: Random House, 1990.

North, Oliver, with William Novak. *Under Fire: An American Story.* New York: HarperCollins, 1991.

O'Neill, Tip, with William Novak. *Man of the House: The Life and Political Memoirs of Speaker Tip O'Neill.* New York: Random House, 1987.

Phillips, Kevin. *The Politics of Rich and Poor, Wealth and the American Electorate in the Reagan Aftermath.* New York: Random House, 1990.

Pizzo, Stephen, Mary Fricker, and Paul Muolo. *Inside Job: The Looting of America's Savings and Loans.* New York: McGraw-Hill, 1989.

President's Special Review Board (Tower Commission). *Report of the President's Special Review Board.* Washington, D.C.: Government Printing Office, 1987.

Prestowitz, Clyde V., Jr. *Trading Places: How We Allowed Japan to Take the Lead.* New York: Basic Books, 1988.

Quigley, Joan. *"What Does Joan Say?" My Seven Years as White House Astrologer to Nancy and Ronald Reagan.* New York: Birch Lane Press, 1990.

Reagan, Maureen. *First Father, First Daughter: A Memoir.* Boston, Little Brown, 1989.

Reagan, Michael, with Joe Hyams. *On The Outside Looking In.* Zebra Books, 1988.

Reagan, Nancy, with William Novak. *My Turn, the Memoirs of Nancy Reagan.* New York: Random House, 1989.

Reagan, Ronald. *An American Life.* New York: Simon & Schuster, 1990.

Reagan, Ronald, and Richard C. Hubler. *Where's the Rest of Me? Ronald Reagan Tells His Own Story.* New York: Dell, 1965.

Regan, Donald T. *For the Record, From Wall Street to Washington.* New York: Harcourt Brace Jovanovich, 1988.

Rogin, Michael. *Ronald Reagan, the Movie and Other Episodes in Political Demonology.* Berkeley: University of California Press, 1987.

Schieffer, Rob, and Gary Paul Gates. *The Acting President.* New York: E. P. Dutton, 1989.

Schwartz, Herman. *Packing the Courts: The Conservative Campaign to Rewrite the Constitution.* New York: Macmillan, 1988.

Shilts, Randy. *And the Band Played On: Politics, People and the AIDS Epidemic.* New York: St. Martin's Press, 1987.

Sick, Gary. *October Surprise: American Hostages in Iran and the Election of Ronald Reagan.* New York: Times Books, 1991.

Speakes, Larry, with Robert Pack. *Speaking Out: The Reagan Presidency from Inside the White House.* New York: Charles Scribner's Sons, 1988.

Stockman, David A. *The Triumph of Politics: How the Reagan Revolution Failed.* New York: Harper & Row, 1986.

Talbott, Strobe. *Master of the Game: Paul Nitze and the Nuclear Peace.* New York: Random House, 1990.

Tolchin, Martin and Susan. *Buying into America: How Foreign Money Is Changing the Face of Our Nation.* New York: New York Times Books, 1988.

Traub, James. *Too Good to Be True: The Outlandish Story of Wedtech.* New York: Doubleday, 1990.

Turner, Stansfield. *Terrorism and Democracy.* Boston: Houghton Mifflin, Co., 1991.

U.S. House of Representatives Select Committee to Investigate Covert Arms Transactions with Iran and U.S. Senate Select Committee on Secret Military Assistance to Iran and the Nicaraguan Opposition. *Report of the Congressional Committees Investigating the Iran-Contra Affair.* Washington, D.C.: U.S. Government Printing Office, 1987.

von Damm, Helene. *At Reagan's Side: Twenty Years in the Political Mainstream.* New York: Doubleday, 1989.

Watts, James, with Doug Wead. *The Courage of a Conservative.* New York: Simon & Schuster, 1985.

Weinberger, Caspar. *Fighting for Peace: Seven Critical Years in the Pentagon.* New York: Warner Books, 1990.

Wills, Garry. *Reagan's America.* Garden City, N.Y.: Doubleday, 1985.

Woodward, Bob. *Veil: The Secret Wars of the CIA 1981–1987.* New York: Simon & Schuster, 1987.

Index